W9-CTZ-454

Table of Contents

CHAPTER 1

Rosh Chodesh Nissan

Kabbalistically, there are two beginnings to the year. There is, of course, Rosh Hashanah, in the month of Tishrei. But in the actual sequence of the months, the first one is Nissan, which is considered the head of all the months. Nissan holds greats gifts for us, but we need to understand exactly what is happening during this month to really take advantage of those gifts.

In the Torah—the Five Books of Moses—there is actually no mention at all of the names of the months. It is only in the later biblical writings—in the Books of Esther, Ezra, and Nehemiah—that the names of the months are mentioned for the first time. What does this tell us?

Kabbalistically, names are powerful. The names of the months are a code to their unique energies, and the Talmud says these codes as well as an understanding of the names of the months were not disclosed until after the Babylonian exile.

Yet the kabbalists also teach that the names of the months were given to Moses at Mount Sinai. There, Moses received the written Torah, together with much secret wisdom. *The Zohar*, for instance, was given to Moses at Sinai, although it was not revealed until many centuries later by Rav Shimon bar Yochai. Moses knew that the time had not yet come for *The Zohar* to be disclosed. Similarly, when Moses received the names of the months, the time was not yet right for their revelation.

The Talmud states that the revelation of the names of the months was connected to the Babylonian exile. There was something about the energy of Babylon that brought this about. Something unique took place there so that the names of the months and their energies could be revealed.

The Babylonian exile was also the period in which the names of the angels were revealed. There are no names of angels mentioned in the Torah. Angels, of course, are referred to throughout the Bible, but the specific names of angels—and therefore the specific energies and powers attached to them—were not revealed until after the Babylonian exile. This too, needs to be explained.

To understand the power of Babylon, we need to refer to the story of the Tower of Babel, which was located in that country. At the time of the Tower of Babel, there was a desire on the part of the people of Babylon to bring about destruction and darkness. *The Zohar* tells us that the Babylonians were so unified in this intention that they almost succeeded. As *The Zohar* explains, the only way to break the unity of the Babylonians was to prevent them from understanding each other, so the Creator caused them to speak in different languages. Nevertheless, the people at the time of the Tower of Babel had great (albeit misguided) wisdom and understanding. They understood the energies of the months and the angels, and they wanted to use those energies to generate negativity.

We know that the Tower of Babel was destroyed. But the incredible revelation of power and energy that came with the names of the months and the angels was brought forth to help humankind during this, the darkest time in the history of Babylon. According to one of Kabbalah's most important precepts, once energy is revealed, it always remains, although the structure in which it exists can be transformed. It's important to understand that the revelation of wisdom is a historical as well as a metaphysical process, and the Babylonian exile was a major positive turning point in history, despite the destruction of the Tower. Now, in this month, each of us has the power to connect to the Light that was disclosed during this time.

It's probably not a coincidence that it was in Babylon (known today as Iraq) that this Light was revealed from darkness. Today, this means that when we speak about the names of the months or about the names of the angels, we are connecting in a spiritual way to the positive energy that exists in Iraq.

Now we can begin to understand the coded meaning of the name *Nissan*, which is derived from the Hebrew word *nes*, which uses the letters *Nun* and *Samech*. The word *nes* has two definitions: "miracle" and "to elevate." So just from the name itself, we understand that Nissan is both a month of miracles and a month of elevation, of rising up. This month is an opening from the Creator that allows all of humanity to access miracles. Although there are other times of the year in which there are openings for miracles, the seed of all miracles for the entire year resides in Nissan.

Therefore, as we enter this month, we have the power to draw miracles into our lives. But how can we activate this power?

To explain this, the Rav has always emphasized the importance of consciousness. Consciousness leads to understanding our power. If we doubt our ability to draw miracles into our lives, we will not be able to draw them. So our first lesson for this month is the importance of removing any doubt about our ability to draw miracles into our lives.

The Zohar teaches that the letter *Nun* is an extremely significant letter. To understand this, we can turn to a very powerful kabbalistic prayer called the *Ashrei*, written by King David, the renowned author of the *Book of Psalms*. Everything that King David wrote was divinely inspired; the words were never merely his own.

All the ancient Hebrew letters, except one, are used in the *Ashrei* prayer. Only the *Nun* is excluded. As *The Zohar* explains, this is because *Nun* is the first letter of the Hebrew word *nefilah*, or "falling." In the great connection to the Light that the Ashrei expresses, King David did not wish to inject any energy of falling, whether physical or spiritual. Therefore the *Nun* was left out. However, *The Zohar* also tells us that the Creator gives all those who fall the ability to sustain and elevate. So although the letter *Nun* represents falling, the letter *Samech*, the next letter of the alphabet, elevates those who fall. Clearly, the connection between these two letters is hugely important.

As Rav Ashlag teaches, we cannot rise without first falling. Falling is not a negative thing—if eventually we become elevated. As a matter of fact, falling has within it the seed of the rising up. Therefore, the connection of *Nun* and *Samech*—falling and rising—makes the *Nun* stronger. It validates the falling. If we had the *Samech* alone, that is, the power of elevating without the falling, we would not have true growth. One of the great gifts of this month is the power to fall and rise, to have the *Nun* and *Samech* together.

We cannot rise to the highest levels, we cannot attain the highest connections to the Light, unless we fall. Every time we fall, every time something doesn't go our way, every time something we were hoping for doesn't happen, it's not enough to just say, "I know that something good will happen at the end." We have to actually take joy in the falling. We have to be happy, to understand there is a reason why we are lower than we were before. And that reason is because there is Light to reveal here.

This is why the kabbalists teach that Nissan is the month of elevation and that all redemptions and elevations have their root in this month. It is a month of certainty that Light will come when we rise up. It is also a month of certainty that the Light is here—even now in our falling. Every difficulty is not only a potential for Light, but has Light within itself.

So we now have an understanding of the tremendous gifts that are available in this month: the gift to draw miracles, not only for this month but for the whole year; the gift of Light in falling; and the true revelation of Light even when we're low. We have unlimited potential during Nissan, provided we work for it and develop it. When we do, we will be able to receive the gifts that are available in this amazing month.

CHAPTER 2

Pesach

The holiday of Pesach is a gift of immeasurable power. On Pesach, we are able to receive tremendous Light as a gift from the Creator. There are many things to understand about this holiday; let's familiarize ourselves with some of them.

Usually the effort required in escaping the Negative Side, our *Desire to Receive for the Self Alone*, or ego, is a huge task in which progress is gradual. The power of Pesach, however, allows us to be freed immediately. At Pesach, each of us can instantly break the influence of the Negative Side, regardless of our spiritual level.

The Torah addresses Pesach and the time of the Ten Plagues in Egypt this way: "And God passed over the opening . . . " The Sfat Emet (Rav Yehuda Leib Alter) explains that the Israelites were not ready for the Exodus from Egypt and that the words: "And God passed over the opening" is a reference to the knowledge that when we make an opening "no wider than the eye of a needle," the Creator will open the Supernal Gates for us. But unfortunately, many people cannot create even a small opening, as was the case for the Israelites in Egypt. So when the Torah says: "And God passed over the opening," this means the Creator ignored the requirement for the people to make even a small opening and just opened for them the Supernal Gates. This is a tremendous lesson for those who understand it. This is the secret of Pesach: On Pesach, all of the Supernal Gates are open, even to those of us who are unable to create even a small opening for spirituality on our own.

When we think about our spiritual work, the task can seem overwhelming. After all, we're trying to bring an end to pain and suffering and death as quickly as possible. The importance of the work can be inspiring, but its magnitude can also be discouraging sometimes. At those moments, it is best not to think about how we need to change people or transform the world. Instead, we should just focus on loosening the grip of the Negative Side.

This can seem much more manageable. And in fact, the process of redemption isn't about everyone suddenly becoming perfect. It's about making a small hole in the dam of negativity. Once that's done, the hole will grow larger naturally and eventually the whole dam will come down by itself. The world is waiting for someone to make that first small hole. By the same token, we don't have to instantly purge ourselves of all negativity. Even if we leave a little bit of energy with our

Negative Side, the revelation of the great Light will still come by itself.

On Pesach, we can completely leave behind our *Desire to Receive for the Self Alone*, even though we might not actually be at the spiritual level where this is possible. The power of Pesach makes it possible for us to be freed at once from the control of the *Desire to Receive for the Self Alone*. Just knowing this makes it impossible not to be filled with joy by the immeasurable gift of this holiday.

Pesach is a time to be free of whatever is holding us back, both as individuals and in relationships with others. This makes Pesach an especially good time to take the essential teachings of Kabbalah to heart and to go beyond the boundaries of our own identity in order to share with other people. *The Zohar* teaches that the most valuable lesson a teacher can give a student is the importance of helping those who are in difficulty and darkness. As Karen Berg often says, "If you have a problem in your life and want a solution, go out of yourself and solve somebody else's problem." A key lesson of Pesach is making a commitment to do more than we have done in the past. If we have tried to help one person, we should try now to help ten. If we've tried to help ten, we should now help a hundred.

This connects to a very important reason for our coming together as a large group at Pesach. The connection we can make either individually or in small groups is much more limited than what we can accomplish when we're all together in a large group. Commenting on this phenomenon, Rav Shimon bar Yochai said that there was only one reason why it was possible to reveal the great Light of *The Zohar*: He and the other sages were in complete unity, and it was that unity that allowed the revelation.

Kabbalists teach that the Final Redemption will come about if complete unity can be achieved in even a single place. When this unity happens, the Light we can ignite will be beyond what any of us has even imagined. We ourselves have the ability to bring about the Final Redemption—but only if we do everything we can to make that Redemption our unified purpose.

Rav Brandwein discussed these ideas in two of his letters to the Rav. In one letter, he speaks of the concept of rushing, and more specifically, of the rushing that takes place at Pesach. As Rav Brandwein explains, we call Pesach the night of order (the word *Seder* literally means "order"), yet part of the miracle of Pesach was the fact that it happened so quickly. The Israelites were baking their bread when suddenly they had to depart from Egypt without even time for the bread to rise. Moses had warned that the Redemption would come quickly. It would come so fast that they wouldn't be able to bake bread nor tie their sandals. They wouldn't even be able to close their doors behind them.

After so many years in Egypt, how could the Israelites believe the Exodus would ever happen? They did believe, but they also knew that belief without action is always very limited. The Israelites believed in Moses and Aaron, but they had to find some physical action to strengthen their consciousness, so they started baking *matzot* (unleavened bread).

This is such an important idea. How many of us really believe in the Redemption? And what actions are we taking to strengthen our consciousness of belief so that it becomes certainty? That is why we say, "Here is the bread they ate in Egypt" when we read from the *Haggadah* (the story of Pesach), even though the Torah says that the Israelites ate of the *matzah* only after they had *left* Egypt. The Israelites' consciousness of certainty was Light, and it was that Light that allowed their Redemption.

Since so much of Pesach involves physical actions taking place in a specific prescribed order, I really want to emphasize the importance of consciousness. All these physical actions are expressions of our certainty that the Redemption is going to come. What's more, the Redemption is going to take place in a certain order, which our actions during the *Seder* are intended to manifest. All this can be achieved through the fifteen steps of the *Seder*. This also tells us that the purpose of our actions is to bring order rather than chaos into our lives, which will lead to the removal of all pain and suffering.

We should always keep in mind how powerful we are, and on Pesach, we want to do much more than we would ordinarily expect to do. At this holiday, we have not just the power to bring so much more Light, we also have the tools: physical objects such as wine, unleavened bread, vegetables, eggs, and so on. If we had true vision, we would see the Light of the Creator in the *matzah*. We would see that these physical objects are actually powerful spiritual tools. It's critical to understand each tool and what it does before we use them, because the magnitude of Light we will reveal is dependent on our consciousness. In short, Light is revealed to the exact degree that we know it will be revealed.

To inspire us to move in the direction of unity and appreciation of what we can achieve, I'd like to mention a very beautiful and important teaching from Rav Ashlag's introduction to *Ten Luminous Emanations*. Rav Ashlag is speaking about Psalm 34:8, "Taste and see that God is good," when he expands on the idea that there is a taste, a feeling, a sensory connection to the Light, and only those who have made that connection can really attest to the fact that the Creator is good. Rav Ashlag refers to the concept that a *tzaddik* (a righteous person) is someone who can truly say that God is good, because everything in their life is good. Those who have not yet tasted, really tasted, the physical manifestation of the beauty of the Light of the Creator cannot feel or understand that God is good. They can't really sense the fact that the whole purpose of Creation is to receive what is good.

This concept of tasting is a litmus test of our spiritual progress. How often do we experience this taste? How often do we have a sense of overwhelming joy in the Light of the Creator? To the degree that someone is dominated by the *Desire to Receive for the Self Alone*, he limits the joy he can feel from the Light; he won't be able to see it and he won't be able to taste it. It's impossible to have *Desire to Receive for the Self Alone* and also have a true feeling for the Light.

Our most important desire should be for the taste of the Creator's Light. We need to continually wish for this and aspire to this. How many of us on a regular basis—when we are reading *The Zohar* or praying—really ask the Creator, "Please let me get to the level of tasting the Light?" We should desire this constantly; we should always be asking and begging for the taste of the Light. The purpose of all our spiritual work should be to bring us to a consciousness of constantly sensing the Light. It is an amazing place to arrive at, but without truly desiring the Light and consistently thinking about it, we will never get there.

In our spiritual work, we must continuously remind ourselves that the world will be redeemed and that we can all become *tzaddikim*. Redemption is always remote for negative people, for the simple reason that they believe it is far away. But a righteous person never stops saying, "I know my Redemption will come, and it will come suddenly in a rush." We need to continuously remind ourselves of this.

This awareness of the coming Redemption should be a life-changing lesson. It should influence what we think about all day. We should know that we are going to become *tzaddikim*. The whole purpose of the *Seder* is to awaken that consciousness—and we do so through physical actions, just as the Israelites ate *matzah* in Egypt. We perform the different actions or steps of the Seder to express our consciousness of and certainty that the Redemption is going to come. But how many of us really believe that the world is going to change soon? How many of us really think, "I am going to become a *tzaddik?*" *Tzaddikim* have a bag always packed. When *Maschiach* (the Messiah and the Final Redemption) comes, they want to be ready.

Although the full experience of Pesach is more than most of us can understand, we still need to raise our consciousness to the greatest possible degree. Thankfully, we have Kabbalah and the great teachers of Kabbalah to assist us: Rav Shimon bar Yochai, Rav Isaac Luria, Rav Ashlag, Rav Brandwein, and the Rav. In revealing the Light, as the kabbalists have said, we are standing on the shoulders of others. The more our consciousness unites with theirs, the greater we can become, and the higher we can go.

One of the key points that Rav Brandwein makes in his letters to the Rav is this: We have to learn to manifest the Light completely. We need such a degree of certainty that we can start to live right now as if freedom has already come. We need certainty that we will find ways to manifest whatever it is that we want, and then the manifestation will occur. This is very different from simply waiting for the Redemption to come and waiting to be happy about it. For example in Psalm 35, King David's certainty in the Creator is so great that even when he is in pain and darkness, he is full of joy. He had no doubt the Light was going to come in the end, and because he was full of joy, he was able to manifest that Light.

To manifest true freedom and fulfillment in our lives, we have to start living it now and feeling it now. Certainty is not something that can wait until after we have manifested the Light. We have to live now so that we can create the Vessel into which the Light can enter. We can no longer say, "I'm going to wait for the Light to manifest my potential." If we want the Light, we have to live, think, and feel the manifestation before it occurs. We have to have the same certainty that caused the Israelites to eat the unleavened bread while they were still in Egypt.

As Rav Brandwein further explains in his letters to the Rav, we can manifest certainty when our lives are aligned with the Light of the Creator. Our goal must be on becoming like the Creator. If that is our focus—if that is the core of who we are and the basis of what we do—then living in certainty now will certainly bring the manifestation.

These are two amazing lessons from Rav Brandwein. For us to awaken the Light and to manifest our true potential, we must first experience the certainty that will let us find ways to become who we are meant to be. Secondly, we must make sure that our lives are aligned with the Light of the Creator, with the purpose of sharing.

If we have certainty but our lives are not aligned in sharing, we will not be able to manifest the Light. By the same token, if we are sharing but do not have certainty, we will not be able to manifest the Light. Only if we meet both these requirements will we be able to manifest the infinite freedom and fulfillment available to us. So certainty plus alignment with the Creator are the first two steps. The final step for manifesting the Light involves our pushing ourselves beyond what is comfortable. It means stretching ourselves farther than we normally go.

At Pesach, we are not there just to eat or just to make blessings. We are there to reveal tremendous Light. The more clearly we understand that fact, the more Light we will reveal.

CHAPTER 3

The Omer

Rav Isaac Luria (the Ari) explains that the purpose of studying the Torah is both for the purification of the soul and for the Light that the actual study draws. The reason the Light of the Creator cannot enter us is because our soul has so much negativity and so many *klippot* (shells that capture and cover the Light) surrounding it that the Light of the Creator cannot enter even if It wants to. One of the most powerful ways to remove these shells, these coverings that stop the Light, is by learning Torah and the Bible—and specifically by studying Kabbalah, *The Zohar*, and *Kitvei Ari* (the writings of Rav Isaac Luria).

In his introduction to *Ten Luminous Emanations*, Rav Ashlag discusses the tremendous importance of Kabbalah study. Even if we don't understand what we are learning, he explains, our desire to *understand* is our Vessel to awaken the *Or Makif* (Surrounding Light) that always encircles us, inviting It to enter. Ultimately, when we complete our transformation, all of us will receive the Light that we are destined to receive, but until we are able to draw all that Light into ourselves, all this potential is called Encircling or Surrounding Light.

Rav Ashlag speaks about the *Ten Sfirot* and about the different names of the Vessels and the Lights. When we study Kabbalah, we kindle these Lights to shine into us. Even though we're not ready to receive all the Light that we have awakened, just by continually saying the names of these Vessels of Light, we get a tremendous amount of Light from Above. This helps us reach the ultimate level that we are supposed to reach. The process of *Sfirat HaOmer* (the Counting of the Omer—the forty-nine days between Pesach and Shavuot) is a bit technical, but there is beauty and wisdom in the technical knowledge as well. And again, just the act of study itself draws a tremendous amount of Light to us.

The Counting of the Omer begins on the second day of Pesach and continues all the way until Shavuot. As we know, every holiday and every observance is not just something we do because our forefathers did it. Rather, we observe a given holiday because at that particular moment, a specific Light is being revealed to the world. We do specific things at those particular times because these special opportunities are tools we can use to connect us to the unique Light available at those moments in time.

The things that occur at those moments aren't things we can see with our eyes or perceive with our senses. Yes, there are some people at such a high level that they can actually see and feel what takes place on the spiritual level, but most of us aren't able to do that. But we still need to know what's happening in order to be able to connect and draw the Light. The writings of the Ari and the other great kabbalists allow us to do this.

Now we're going to explore both what the Ari teaches us about the Omer and what's really happening during these forty-nine days.

We know that everything that happens in the physical world is only a manifestation of what is occurring in the spiritual dimension. So in order to accomplish our purpose in this physical world, we have to be able to understand the spiritual powers that control it. For example, we need to understand the *Ten Sfirot*, the *Ten Luminous Emanations* of the Creator's Light.

To achieve this understanding, we begin with the fact that the Light is endless. But there's a problem. We're living in a physical world in which the Vessels that receive the Light are of various sizes. How does the Light get down to us? And how does the infinite Light of the Creator enter our limited and finite Vessels? The Light can't confine or restrict Itself; there needs to be a *tzimtzum*, a withdrawal, a constriction of the Light for It to be available to us.

So we're not dealing with the totality of the Light. We can't connect to the totality as long as we're living in this world, which is why we have the constriction of the Light and the *Ten Sfirot*. The *Sfirot* are the channels that filter the Light that comes down into this world, putting the Light through constriction after constriction so It can enter our Vessels. This works much the way step-down transformers reduce the power from a nuclear power plant before it enters our home as electricity.

Each of the *Ten Sfirot* deals with a different amount of Light, or a different type of energy. And each of the *Ten Sfirot* draws Light from the *Sfirah* above it, until we get down to the *Sfirah* of *Malchut*, the physical world, which has the smallest amount of Light. A lower *Sfirah* cannot receive the full Light of the *Sfirah* above it; it can only receive constricted Light. We connect to *Malchut*, which gives us our best chance to not be overwhelmed by the Creator's Light.

(As an aside, I want to mention that although we generally speak of *Ten Sfirot*, we sometimes also speak of an eleventh, which is known as Da'at. To explain this, the Ari writes that each group of *Sfirot* needs to have three columns—Right, Left, and Central. But the highest group of *Sfirot—Keter*, *Chochmah*, and *Binah*—did not have a Central Column. Da'at, which contains the collective attributes of the Light of *Zeir Anpin*, is introduced to act as the stabilizing Central Column between the Light of *Chochmah* and *Binah*.)

Chochmah and *Binah* are called Supernal Father and Supernal Mother, respectively, because they are the source of all the Light that we receive. Like a child who gets everything from his or her parents, we get all the Light that we need from *Chochmah* and *Binah*. We need to have both sides, father and mother, right and left—that is the only way we can receive the Light.

When we speak of Pesach, which is the beginning of the Omer, we have to understand that when the Israelites were in Egypt, they were at the lowest possible spiritual level from which there could be no return. Every generation kept descending to a lower and lower level until by the time of Moses, the Israelites were at the lowest possible level. The Creator understood that if the Israelites were left in this condition, they would be totally destroyed in a spiritual sense.

Therefore, the Creator had to come up with a miracle to get them out of this downward destructive spiral. The Creator had to give them so much Light that all their negativity would fall away. In very simple terms, that is the miracle of Pesach. All the Light that was possible was given to the Israelites at that one time. What then happened was the same thing that happens if a person is holding onto a metal pot and suddenly that pot is filled with extremely hot water. The heat of the water is transmitted through the handle of the pot, and whoever is holding onto the pot will let go. In much the same way, the Israelites were in slavery in Egypt, and the sudden influx of Light forced the Egyptians to let them go. On the first night of Pesach, all this Light was revealed, and all the negativity that was keeping the Israelites in bondage went away.

But as *The Zohar* and the Ari explain, there was a problem. Kabbalah teaches that you cannot keep something that you have not earned. The people of Israel had not earned that Light, so almost all the negativity that they had before came rushing back.

This brings us to the whole meaning of the Omer and of our work during this time, which is to *earn back* the Light that we received for free on the first night of Pesach and that we lost as a result. On Shavuot, we are going to again be getting all the Light that we originally received on Pesach, but this time the Light will be ours to keep. Now that we have done the work that allows us to receive the Light through our own efforts, we will actually achieve a higher level.

But a question could be asked: If all our negativity returned after Pesach, what was the purpose of Pesach in the first place? If we have to eventually work for the Light anyway, how are we helped by receiving the Light for free?

The Ari explains that even though the negativity does come back, its hold over us is not as strong as it was before. If the people had retained the same consciousness as they had before Pesach, they could never have accomplished the work of drawing back the Light. Accomplishing that work of drawing back the Light is what we're doing right now through the Counting of the Omer.

Kabbalistically, what happened in Egypt was that the people had destroyed their Vessels. They had to rebuild those Vessels, which is exactly what we need to do during this time of the Omer. This is the only way we can come to Shavuot and enjoy the Light of Immortality that is available. But how do we do this?

Everything spiritual has to go through four levels of growth. The Ari explains, for example, that a child is at one level until he's nine years old; at another level when he is thirteen; at yet another level at twenty-one; and finally beyond twenty-one, at a fourth level. So too, are there levels of growth during the Omer. The most important task that we have during the Omer is to rebuild our Vessels until we reach the point that we can again receive the Light of the Creator at Shavout. We have forty-nine days—seven weeks—in the Omer. Each of these weeks is actually devoted to rebuilding one of the six *Sfirot* of *Zeir Anpin* plus the *Sfirah* of *Malchut*.

When all the six *Sfirot* of *Zeir Anpin* are corrected along with Malchut and once all the Vessels are rebuilt, we can begin receiving the Light in our physical world.

The more we understand this, the more we can do, which in turn allows us to receive more Light. The more we know, the more we have to know. The more we do, the more we have to do. We have to push ourselves. The amount of Light we receive is based on the amount of spiritual work we do.

There is a story of a great kabbalist who had a large number of students. One day, the students met a man who had just returned from a distant country where he had gotten very rich. This gave the students an idea: Maybe they could take some time off from their Torah studies to go to that country. Then, after they made a lot of money, they could return to study in luxury.

When they told their teacher about this plan, he had another suggestion. He told his students, "If you want to get rich, there's no need to go anywhere. You can do that right here." Then he led them to the top of a high mountain. As they looked into the valley below, the kabbalist said, "If you wish, I can fill this entire valley with gold and you can take as much as you want. You can instantly be rich. But there's one condition. As your riches grow, the level of your soul will diminish."

Not one of the students accepted this offer. They had studied enough Kabbalah to know that anything worth having must be earned and worked for. In the same way, the Omer is a time for doing the spiritual work that earns the Light of Shavuot. This is a hugely exciting opportunity, and we need to take full advantage of it.

CHAPTER 4

Rosh Chodesh Iyar

The kabbalists call this month Iyar, spelled *Alef, Yud, Yud, Reish*. These letters are a coded message that reveals the month's internal energy. The word *Iyar* is actually an acronym for *Ani Hashem Rofecha* (I, God, am your healer). During Iyar, therefore, we receive the gift of true and lasting healing.

As the Rav has repeatedly made clear, our first understanding in this month must be the knowledge that we *do* have the ability to heal ourselves, not only on the physical level but also emotionally, and certainly spiritually. True, we might need assistance and we might go to a doctor to help us in the healing process, but real and lasting healing power originates inside

25

each of us. Ultimately, to bring about permanent healing, we need to connect with healing Light, and the *knowledge* that we *can* heal ourselves is the connection for bringing the Light of healing permanently into our lives.

We must always remind ourselves that every form of chaos—including illness—is an illusion and will not last. This is the most important awareness we need to have when facing any sort of chaos in our lives. We must persevere based on our consciousness that chaos is only a physical manifestation and therefore temporary. Its disappearance may not come quickly or easily, but in the end, the illusion that is chaos *will* vanish.

When we read from the writings of the great kabbalists, we not only gain their wisdom but also connect to their energy, including the energy of healing that is available during the month of Iyar. So it's important not simply to explain the ideas that the kabbalists teach but also to actually connect to the words of their teachings. The Light is in those words.

Rav Yehuda Ashlag, founder of The Kabbalah Centre, speaks about the tools we need to awaken this healing process from within. Rav Ashlag asks, "Why did the kabbalists say that it is important for every single person to study *The Zohar*?" There are many spiritual teachings in the world, but kabbalists speak about *The Zohar* in a way that's very different from other teachings. The kabbalists were adamant about the fact that everybody needs to have access to this wisdom. Rav Ashlag asks why this is true. Why is this wisdom so essential?

He answers by saying, "There is a very important idea here. No matter who you are, studying *The Zohar* is a tremendous gift and a tremendous merit. Even if a person only scans *The Zohar* and finds it impossible to understand, the act of scanning in itself has tremendous power. The connection itself, even when not understood, awakens the Light that surrounds our soul."

As Rav Ashlag goes on to explain, every single one of us will achieve our *tikkun* (correction). Every single one of us will finish what we came into this world to accomplish. We will achieve spiritual perfection and complete connection to the Light of the Creator and to ultimate fulfillment. This is guaranteed for every single one of us. The only question is how long and how difficult that process will be for each individual human being. But that is something within our control.

What the Creator desires is a world in which there is no pain, where there is no suffering, and where every single one of us has complete connection to the Light. This is the true Thought of Creation, and that purpose will be achieved. It's guaranteed. If people do not merit it in this incarnation, then they'll correct it in the next one. If they don't correct it in the next one, they'll come back again. The length of the process and the difficulty of the process are up to us, but the end of the process is certain. Every single one of us will achieve perfection.

As long as we have not yet achieved our perfection, as long as we are still lacking that complete connection to the Light of the Creator through our spiritual work, then all the Light that we haven't brought into our life yet is known as *Or Makif* (Surrounding Light), and it literally surrounds our souls.

The Light that we have internalized and that gives us a certain degree of fulfillment, the kabbalists call *Or Pnimi*, or Inner Light. It is the Light that we have gained through our work, and it is the joy that we feel in our lives. But it's not complete. For many of us, it's not lasting. Every single one of us has moments when we are disconnected from the Light. Why?

We haven't done the work to be able to internalize our Surrounding Light, our potential Light.

Every single one of us walks around with two sets of Light. *Or Pnimi*, the Inner Light, is what we've already accomplished: To some degree, we have already transformed ourselves from having a selfish *Desire to Receive* to embracing the *Desire to Share*. The second Light, the Surrounding Light, *Or Makif*, is the Light that surrounds our souls, waiting and begging for us to bring it in and to achieve true and lasting fulfillment. When the kabbalists talk about Surrounding Light, they're talking about all the joy and fulfillment that every single one of us is meant to achieve and will achieve.

Once we transform completely, once we elevate and purify ourselves and our Vessels, then that Surrounding Light can become internalized. Until we've transformed, the Light is there but the Vessel is not yet ready. This is one of the most important teachings of Kabbalah: The Light is always available, but the Vessel is lacking. As we transform further, as we remove more of our ego, we create a larger and larger Vessel for the Surrounding Light.

This is the beauty of the lesson that Rav Ashlag teaches. When a person studies Kabbalah, when a person connects to *The Zohar* and to the teachings of the kabbalists, immediately that Light shines into him or her. Rav Ashlag says that when we read and connect to *The Zohar* and speak its words, we awaken those aspects of our Surrounding Light that correspond to that section in *The Zohar*. And by doing that, Rav Ashlag explains, we are able to draw an element of that Light and connect to it. So when we connect to *The Zohar*, we are actually awakening our own potential. From this, it is clear that everything we do at The Kabbalah Centre—all the books we publish and all the classes we teach—are important because it brings us to a stronger connection with the Light of the Creator.

Some time ago, I had a dream about the importance of this understanding. In the dream, the Rav came to me and said, "For all these years I've been saying that it is all about *The Zohar*, and nobody really understands it." The Rav was underscoring the value of our work at The Centre, but he was also saying something more specific: Real change can come about only by using the tool of *The Zohar*. If we hope to end chaos in our world, we must use *The Zohar*.

The problem most of us have in our spiritual work is a lack of excitement and the desire to truly grow, to truly change. But why? It's because our Surrounding Light is dormant. That Light, our potential, cries out to us all the time: "Manifest me! Bring this lasting fulfillment that you already have around you into your life!" But unfortunately, every time we act in a negative or selfish manner, every time we act in anger, we are refusing the potential of our own Surrounding Light.

How can we make ourselves understand the importance of a continual connection to this wisdom?

If you look at *The Zohar* or Kabbalah as another way to understand the world around you or to understand your life, you're functioning on an important spiritual level, but it is *not* the one that will bring you to your true purpose in life. If you want to achieve your true purpose in life, it has to be with this understanding: When you open *The Zohar*, you want to awaken your Surrounding Light. No matter what section you open in *The Zohar*, no matter what lesson you are learning in Kabbalah, that awakening is your singular purpose. You need to know that you are awakening the Surrounding Light, and that this Light is shining into you and awakening your true desire for change and growth. As Rav Ashlag says, when we receive this Light time and time again, we awaken in ourselves an abundance of Light and holiness. Even if we don't understand a single word of *The Zohar*, that Light pushes us towards transformation and change.

The first lesson we should take into the month of Iyar—this month of wisdom, this month of understanding and healing—is this amazing teaching from Rav Ashlag. Don't study Kabbalah just because it gives you understanding, although that's certainly a great thing. Study Kabbalah; make a consistent connection to *The Zohar* and to this wisdom, because you need to awaken your Surrounding Light. If you don't continuously awaken your Surrounding Light, your potential for lasting fulfillment will remain dormant.

On a deeper level, Rav Yehuda Brandwein, a student of Rav Ashlag and teacher of the Rav, said, "Who among us wouldn't want to really be able to feel, to see, to have this divine inspiration, to know the right thing to do, to know the right thing to say? The only way we can achieve this is by connection to our own soul." This means connection to *Etz Chaim*, the Tree of Life, where there are no ups and downs, where there is only lasting fulfillment. In other words, what Rav Brandwein means is: "Forget about even the Surrounding Light. Your own soul, the Light that you've already internalized, will not be awakened if you're not constantly awakening it."

If we give up, if we simply forget about awakening our soul and just live within our bodies, we live in the realm of the Tree of Knowledge of Good and Evil with its ups and downs, its positives and negatives. But we have the ability to truly connect to the *Etz Chaim* through the experience of study.

Again, the word "study" is limiting because we're not just referring to intellectual understanding. This studying is a tool to awaken the soul so that our actions, our words, and our thoughts are truly of the Tree of Life.

Many people who come to The Kabbalah Centre study for years. Others are here for much shorter periods of time. People come and go, but whether someone stays or not, it is important to remember what lies at the core of The Kabbalah Centre's work—and at the core of the wisdom of Kabbalah. Ultimate fulfillment is our destiny. Chaos is not permanent. This is a tremendous gift for us during the month of Iyar. It's a gift of connection through the tool of study, but it must be study with the consciousness of awakening our soul.

Now when we open *The Zohar*, it's because we know that we cannot leave our soul dormant any longer. As the kabbalists teach, the true purpose of wisdom is not to accumulate information but to awaken our soul and to awaken our Surrounding Light. The gift of this month is that the Gates of Heaven are open, not just now but for the entire year.

CHAPTER 5

Lag B'Omer

Whenever great souls depart this world, the energy of their souls is awakened every year on the anniversary of their departure. Therefore this day—the thirty-third day of the Omer, known as Lag B'Omer, and the anniversary of Rav Shimon bar Yochai's passing—is one of the most powerful days of the year in terms of connection to what the kabbalists call "the perfect world."

What is meant by "the perfect world"? Rav Ashlag tells us that before this world began, the Thought of Creation already existed in the mind of God: the vision of a world without pain, suffering, or chaos; a world of ultimate fulfillment and joy. The

33

Light of that perfect world was revealed by Rav Shimon in *The Zohar*. Indeed, the Light of the perfect world is *The Zohar's* essence. Every year on this day, the Light of Lag B'Omer is awakened, and by connecting to that Light, we connect to the essence of what Rav Shimon revealed. We connect to the perfect world for each of us as individuals and for all humankind as well.

On this anniversary of Rav Shimon's passing, we connect not only with Rav Shimon's great soul but also to the Thought of Creation, the seed of the perfect world that *The Zohar* embodies. To maximize that connection, we can read *The Zohar's* account of Rav Shimon leaving this world. As we do so, we need to be aware that this is not merely about an event that took place a couple of thousand years ago, nor is *The Zohar's* account, a description. When we read the pages of *The Zohar*, we are living this sacred event. It is occurring for us now, every bit as powerfully as it did 2000 years ago.

On the day that Rav Shimon chose to leave this world, he achieved such a level of connection to the Light that even the Angel of Death had no power over him. Rav Shimon chose to leave on this day because he knew the world needed his revelation. Gathered around him were Rav Elazar, his son, Rav Aba, and other students and friends. As Rav Shimon saw that his whole house was full of people, he wept and said, "Once, when I was ill, only my father-in-law, Rav Pinchas ben Yair, was with me. Now it seems that anyone can enter without any respect to me."

At that moment, Rav Shimon saw that a fire had surrounded his house. As the fire appeared, everyone departed. Only his son, Rav Elazar, and Rav Aba were still present; all the other students were now sitting outside. Then Rav Shimon turned to his son and instructed him to find the group of sages known as "the friends." These were the sages who had been present with Rav Shimon at the *Idra Raba* (the Greater Assembly) as he revealed *The Zohar*'s Light.

When Rav Elazar had gathered the friends, Rav Shimon stood up. He was smiling and happy. *The Zohar* makes the point strongly that Rav Shimon was full of joy as he raised his hands and prayed. And once again, it's important to remind ourselves that we are not simply hearing a story but rather we are reawakening this Light. These events are happening now as we read or hear about them.

Rav Shimon said, "This day, the thirty-third day of the Omer, is a day of great openings and tremendous desire. The Gates of the Supernal World are open." He continued, "It is my desire to go up to the Supernal World with no secrets left unrevealed in the physical world. The great secrets that I have not revealed, I want to reveal now. It cannot be said that I left this world without every secret being revealed."

When Rav Shimon spoke of "secrets," he did not mean wisdom or deeper understanding. He meant the revelation of another layer of Light. Ultimately, the Light he revealed on the day he left this world—and that he is revealing again now as we connect to this telling—encompasses all the Light that we are lacking. Yet, as Rav Ashlag writes, although Rav Shimon's Light is revealed today, each of us still has to create a personal opening, a Vessel to receive that Light. The revelation of Light that we need—and that the world needs—is awakened on Lag B'Omer, but it is incumbent on every single one of us also to personally reveal that Light in our life.

The Zohar describes how Rav Shimon directed the sages who were with him. He said, "Rav Aba will be the scribe. My son,

Rav Elazar, shall repeat my words as I say them. And the other students should repeat the words in their heart." Rav Aba, who had been sitting behind Rav Shimon, now rose to sit in front of him. Rav Shimon said to his son, "Make a place for Rav Aba to sit in front of me." Rav Shimon covered Rav Aba's head completely as he Rav Aba sat down.

Rav Shimon began to speak a verse from the Book of Psalms that says that the dead cannot reveal the Light; they can assist us, but the actual revelation must be done by the living. Then he went on to describe how different this day was from the first revelation, known as the Greater Assembly, when as he revealed *The Zohar*, many of the angels were present. Rav Shimon said, "This day is different, and it is greater. Not only is the Creator present, but all the souls of the righteous and all of the angels as well. Every righteous soul that has ever lived is also here to support this great revelation."

Rav Aba recounts that Rav Shimon went on to reveal all the concealed Light that he had not earlier revealed. Rav Shimon spoke the verse: "There the Creator left the blessing, eternal life." As Rav Shimon ended this verse there was silence.

(As an aside, we know that Rav Ashlag, who actually completed the revelation of *The Zohar*, spoke almost the same words when he, too, left this world on Yom Kippur in 1954.)

Rav Aba said, "I couldn't raise my head because the Light was so great in the room. I could not look. I had to close my eyes. I was shaken. I heard a heavenly voice that called out and said, 'Let there be days and years of life.' And then I heard another voice saying, 'He asked for life, and He gave it to him.'"

Now the fire that had earlier surrounded Rav Shimon's house surrounded his bed, and this fire was so great that no one could approach. Rav Aba and the other friends fell to the floor. They tried to stand but were too weak. Finally, the fire departed and Rav Aba said, "I saw the Holy of Holies that left this world." Rav Shimon was lying on his left side and he was smiling. His son, Rav Elazar, stood up, took the hands of his father and kissed them. Rav Aba was kissing the ground at the feet of Rav Shimon. The friends wanted to weep but couldn't make a sound. Rav Elazar fell on the floor three times. At first he couldn't speak, but as he gathered strength he said, "Father, father, there used to be three great souls in the world: Rav Pinchas ben Yair, Rav Shimon, and Rav Elazar. Only Rav Elazar remains."

Then Rav Aba stood and said, "Until now Rav Shimon took care of us. Now it is time for us to take care of him." Rav Elazar and Rav Aba stood up and began carrying the bed of Rav Shimon. *The Zohar* writes that what then took place cannot be imagined. The entire house was filled with beautiful scents. No one else touched Rav Shimon, only Rav Aba and Rav Elazar. They said, "Come and enjoy the feast, the great day of Rav Shimon. Come in peace. Rav Shimon, rest in your resting place. Rav Shimon is that soul from which the Creator draws joy every day. Worthy is his place in the Supernal World and in our world!"

It bears repeating once again that as we read this story, we are reawakening this Light right here and now. Each of us will connect to it in a different way, but through sheer desire and appreciation, we can maximize our connection with Rav Shimon on Lag B'Omer.

The Zohar tells us that wherever Rav Shimon was, no judgment could be present. His soul was unique. Moses was able to reveal the literal Torah, but only the soul of Rav Shimon could reveal the secrets. He had the ability to make tremendous Supernal Light accessible to all of us. Moses revealed the Light that was above, and Rav Shimon was able to take the highest Light and reveal it to us in the physical world. We need about the passing of Rav Shimon in *The Zohar* to make our connection to that Light, and for this reason, Lag B'Omer is greater than almost any other day of the year. On Lag B'Omer, Rav Shimon reveals the Light from the perfect world. Our task is to desire and appreciate this connection.

So much Light is concealed in *The Zohar,* and so much Light is concealed in the soul of Rav Shimon. Now, on Lag B'Omer, we have the complete revelation of *The Zohar* as well as the Light of the soul of Rav Shimon. It is a tremendous day.

Lag B'Omer is the perfect time of year to clarify the purpose of Zohar study. Specifically, I would like to address one very important point: Even if we don't know how to pronounce the Aramaic words, we can still draw a great amount of Light just by scanning *The Zohar.* But we must never forget the importance of doing the most that we can. If we can't read, we should scan. If we can read, we should also try to speak the words aloud, without worrying about mispronouncing them. If we can speak the words aloud, we should do so as often as we can.

The Zohar, written by Rav Shimon bar Yochai almost 2000 years ago, contains a great amount of knowledge about Kabbalah and other topics. Nevertheless, *The Zohar* is much more than an intellectual masterpiece. On our spiritual path, even for those of us who truly want to climb great spiritual heights, we may feel that the Negative Side is stronger than we are and that we are too weak to overcome our ego's desires. Even though we may understand that those desires are negative and destructive, we feel we are unable to defeat them. Furthermore, we are often blind in a spiritual sense, confused about the right thing to do.

The source for both the lack of strength to fight the Negative Side, and our spiritual blindness is the same. The Hebrew word for this source is *klippot*, the shells that encapsulate our Light and which we have brought upon ourselves through our negative actions, both in this incarnation and in previous ones. As long as these shells cover us, we cannot attain the spiritual level that we came to this world to achieve; we cannot advance toward fulfillment.

When revealing *The Zohar*, Rav Shimon not only disclosed tremendous secrets but also instilled in *The Zohar*'s very words a supernatural cleansing power. Once we understand this, the purpose of *The Zohar* becomes clear: It is to cleanse our spiritual klippot. For this reason, we should read *The Zohar* every single day. Without *The Zohar*, it is extremely difficult—if not impossible—to achieve true spiritual transformation. As Rav Ashlag said, "The gift is in front of all of us. We should use it!"

CHAPTER 6

Rosh Chodesh Sivan

The month of Sivan, whose sign is Gemini (the twins), expresses the concept that just as there is positive, there is also negative; just as there is right, there is also left. There is always an exact balance.

The great Kabbalist Rav Isaac Luria (the Ari) clarified this duality that exists in all of us for his student, Rav Chaim Vital. As Rav Luria explained, "You have one of the greatest souls that ever came into this world. But because you have such a great soul, you also have a great darkness to overcome. Within you there is an exact balance of good and evil."

The Ari told Rav Chaim Vital that his particular great darkness took the form of anger. Chaim Vital's anger was as great as his Light. To truly manifest the greatness of his soul, Rav Vital needed to be able to defeat the anger within him.

Even in the greatest souls, there is a balance of good and evil, of positive and negative, of darkness and Light. When we see darkness in ourselves, we should not be surprised. Instead, we should look at how we can change. We should also realize that darkness within us is just a sign that we have tremendous potential to reveal Light. If we perform a negative action, we should say to ourselves, "I'm not going to be upset with myself now. I'm going to realize that if I could do something so negative, I also have the ability to do something remarkably positive that can reveal even more Light."

This is one of the most important kabbalistic lessons. The Negative Side will say to us, "Look at what you've done! Look at the darkness you have brought!" If we listen to that voice, we will become depressed and without hope. In fact, just listening to it at all is yet another negative action.

King Solomon was deeply connected to wisdom and Light, yet King Solomon wrote that real wisdom can come only from folly. *The Zohar* tells the story of a kabbalist, one of the great sages of *The Zohar*, who would always have one of his students say something humorous or even silly before he began teaching.

There was another great kabbalist whose students would pray with him, and afterwards, as if by magic, he would tell his students what they had prayed for. He would also tell them whether what they had asked for would actually be granted.

One Yom Kippur he told a student, "I saw that you wanted time to study, pray, and meditate rather than having to work for a living. So on the eve of Yom Kippur you asked the Creator for money to live on during the coming year. But the next morning you had a different prayer. You said to God, 'If you give me money right at the beginning of the year, I might get involved in investing it and worrying about it. Instead, perhaps you can give me half of the money that I need in the beginning of the year, and then the second half in the middle of the year. That way my year will be free for spiritual work.'"

"But in the afternoon prayer," the kabbalist continued, "you changed your mind again. Your request this time was for quarterly payments!" Then the kabbalist concluded, "Do you know what the Heavens answered? The Heavens said, 'Do you think the Creator desires for you to pray and to meditate all year? That's not what the Creator wants. He wants you to live and work in the world, even if it's working in a tavern or collecting garbage. You might have only a few minutes for prayer, but the Light that emerges from the darkness around you will be greater than all the Light you could reveal if you prayed all day, because we're in this world to reveal Light from darkness and to reveal wisdom from folly.'"

According to a kabbalistic saying, "God has angels in Heaven. He doesn't need angels in the world." The Creator needs people who do both bad and good—people who will first reveal darkness but then, out of the darkness, they will reveal Light. That is the first lesson of this month and one of the most important.

A second aspect of Sivan deals with the concept of bribes. The Torah says we should not accept bribes. But if we read the Torah literally, it seems that this section pertains specifically to judges. Judges should not take bribes from people coming to court. However, since every word of the Torah speaks to every single one of us, kabbalists explain that we frequently bribe ourselves. We engage in positive actions; we share; we reveal Light. Then when we do something negative, we say, "True, I've perpetrated a negative action, but look at all the good I'm doing! Look at all the Light I'm revealing! Look at all the connections I'm making!"

Such thinking is nothing more than a bribe. Whenever we allow our Light to overshadow our consciousness of our own darkness, we are bribing ourselves. We are buying ourselves off and allowing ourselves to compromise.

In the commentaries on the Torah that concern Sivan and its sign of Gemini, there is a very interesting story concerning Rebecca, the wife of Isaac and the mother of the twins, Jacob and Esau. When Rebecca was pregnant, one of the twins would want to jump out of her womb whenever she walked past a place of positive energy. And whenever she passed a negative place, the other child would want to be born. But Rebecca did not know she was bearing twins. She thought it was one child who didn't know whether he wanted to be positive or negative, whether he was excited by the Light of the Creator or by darkness.

She was very worried so she went to one of the great kabbalists of the time and told him about her concern. The kabbalist said, "Don't worry. You have two children in your womb. One, Jacob, will connect to the Light of the Creator, and the other, Esau, will connect to darkness."

I think most parents would rather have had one child who is like the rest of us—sometimes connected to the Light and sometimes to darkness, sometimes to right and sometimes to wrong. But Rebecca was happy to hear that one son was going to be completely righteous and one son was going to be completely negative.

We can understand this in two ways. We can believe Rebecca was happy to be the parent of a great, righteous soul like Jacob. But kabbalists propose that Rebecca was happy for Esau also. She knew that as long as a person was connecting to both the Light and the darkness, then they might be a good person but they might also never achieve the purpose for which they came to this world. But if someone is completely negative, if everything this person does is only for the Negative Side, then he or she has a chance. One day they might say, "Look what I've done with my life. I've never revealed any Light. I've only created darkness for myself and for those around me." Then they can *truly* desire connection with the Light. But when we are in the middle, when we are mediocre, when we are sometimes connecting to the Light and sometimes connecting to darkness, we will never have a chance to become awakened.

In this month of Gemini, it is a tremendous lesson that Rebecca teaches us concerning her twin sons. Our Light should not bribe us to accept our darkness. Mediocrity will never lead us to a complete connection to the Light of the Creator. The lesson of this month is to *not* stay in the middle, to not accept the bribe of our own positive actions. If we compromise our connection to the Light, we compromise the blessings we can bring into our life. We came into this world to achieve a *complete* connection to the Light of the Creator, which can only occur if we don't accept the bribe from our own Negative Side.

If we maximize the opportunity of this month, if we truly use the lessons of Gemini, we will not only reveal tremendous Light but we will also transform our darkness. *The Zohar* tells us that by transforming negative energies into Light we can bring about the end of pain and suffering both in our own lives and in the world as a whole. This understanding—and the power to transform this understanding into action—is the amazing gift of this month of Sivan.

CHAPTER 7

Shavuot

Our connection to the Light of Shavuot is unique, totally different from any other connection that we make throughout the year. As the kabbalists explain, this is the one time of the year we actually connect to *Gamar Hatikkun*, the end of the correction process and the Final Redemption.

There is a powerful section in *The Zohar* called "The Night of the Bride." I believe this is the only section where Rav Ashlag, the greatest kabbalist of our century and the translator of the entire *Zohar*, offers two different explanations and understandings for a single section of *The Zohar*. It is a long and beautiful section, and as we read it, we can appreciate the tremendous gift that is available at Shavuot.

The Zohar describes Rav Shimon bar Yochai sitting and studying on the Night of the Bride, a time when the energy of the bride comes together with that of her husband, the night when the male and female principle completely unite. In *The Zohar*, we learn of all the people who come together at this time to connect to the tremendous revelation of Light of the "wedding," which will take place the following morning. These people also desire to partake of the Light that is present with the Bride the night before her wedding. This is the Light that prepares her for her connection—and that prepares us to read and study the Torah (Five Books of Moses), the Prophets, the Ketuvim (Writings) of the Kings, and the Megilot (Books). These sections form twenty-four books.

As we will see, at the end of each of these books there is a two-letter Hebrew combination. Those letters are considered the jewelry, the adornment for the bride. They are the preparation for the great union. The union occurs the next day, but the spiritual work is done the evening before. *The Zohar* makes this very clear. The reading of the twenty-four books and the meditation on the twenty-four combinations at the end of each reading prepare the bride for the union—for the Light that will be revealed in the morning at the marriage, the coming together of *Zeir Anpin* and *Malchut*, the Upper and Lower Worlds.

Rav Ashlag's discussion of this is very exciting and very powerful. We learn that this section of *The Zohar* has two different explanations that join together, like rivers that empty into the same sea.

The time in which we now live is called "night" because there is still pain and suffering in the world. This is a time when the Light of the Creator is not completely revealed. Negativity can still attach itself to us. But in this time there is also the potential power to create the union of male and female that will bring about, as Rav Ashlag describes, the *Gamar Hatikkun*, the Final Correction. The Bride represents the preparation of humanity for the end of the correction, a time when pain and suffering will be removed from this world. The Groom represents the Light of the Creator. As *The Zohar* explains, this is the moment when pain and suffering will be removed from our world forever.

The second explanation concerns the actual night of Shavuot (Erev Shavuot), which we connect to and participate in each year. This night is the time we have already discussed, when the Bride, who is *Malchut*, is being prepared for union in the morning with her Groom, who is *Zeir Anpin*.

These are two different explanations, two different ways to understand this section of *The Zohar*. One of them is the big picture of the world that is still filled with pain and suffering, and the other is the union and coming together of the Bride and the Groom that will ultimately bring the *Gamar Hatikkun*, which is the morning that *The Zohar* is speaking about.

As Rav Ashlag says, both these explanations are actually one. The day of Shavuot, when the Light of the Torah was revealed thousands of years ago on Mount Sinai, is a revelation of the *Gamar Hatikkun* that occurs every year when, as the Bible says, death will be swallowed up. It occurred then, thousands of years ago, and we have to understand that this day of Shavuot is the one time of the year when the Light to remove pain and suffering from the world is completely revealed again. As Rav Ashlag says, whether we understand it to be the final removal of pain and suffering or just the removal of pain and suffering for this day only, both are the same. Now is a time for every one of us to remove pain and suffering from our lives—and also to remove pain and suffering from the world as a whole.

Every holiday holds different connections and different opportunities. Yom Kippur, Pesach, and Rosh Hashanah are about how to make the coming year better. But this connection at Shavuot has a different potential: It is about how we can make *eternity* better. That is the opportunity we have at Shavuot. That is the purpose of what we are doing by staying up all night and connecting to the twenty-four books.

It's important that we don't lose our consciousness and our awareness of what this means. As we are listening to the words of the reading and meditating on the combinations of letters and sounds, we can ignite in our consciousness a real understanding of the connection that we are being given. Every one of us will connect in a different way, depending on our energy and our understanding. To the degree we connect with the Light, we will reveal Light.

As we read in *The Zohar* about Rav Shimon at Shavuot, every one of us can partake of the connection he made then—and that he makes at this time every year. *The Zohar* describes how Rav Shimon and his students were singing and joyfully making a connection with the Torah. Rav Shimon said, "My children, worthy is your share. Tomorrow in the morning, there will be an amazing union of the Supernal Male and Supernal Female. You will be able partake of that Light, and of that energy, because all those who partake of this preparation enable the Supernal Bride and Groom to come together."

The stronger our preparations, the more Light we will reveal for ourselves and for the world. Rav Shimon says that not only do we need to make the connection but we must also be full of joy as we make these preparations. Those of us who have the merit to make connections with joy and consciousness will be blessed with seventy blessings.

Then Rav Shimon goes on to explain, "When the Bride goes into marriage the next morning, into the union, she will bring with her all those friends—all of us—who have been with her during the night of her preparation." The Night of the Bride is an amazing section of *The Zohar*. I highly recommend that everyone read it on the night of Shavuot.

Towards the end of the night, Rav Shimon says, "Let us sit now and prepare the Bride on this night. Whoever takes part with her in the preparation during this night will be protected in our world and in the Upper World for the year to come. We will live this year in peace. For the Creator sends His angels to protect those who merit to make this connection. Those who make this connection can achieve the level of being able to completely connect and feel the Light of the Creator."

I would also like to discuss the writings of Rav Isaac Luria, *Kitvei Ari*, that relate to this section. The Ari quotes from *The Zohar*: "You should know that whoever does not sleep on this night, even for one moment, and listens to the readings of the Torah, will be protected throughout the year." As the Ari says, not only can we gain protection by making this connection and by not sleeping even for a moment on this night, but a person who does not sleep at all will not die during the coming year.

If we appreciate what *The Zohar* is revealing to us about this night, every one of us has the opportunity to partake in this union that does not occur at any other time of the year. Through our joy and through the power of our connection, we have the ability to bring about the Final Correction. And even if we don't completely bring it about, we can at least move in that direction. What happens, Erev Shavuot is about what will happen during the entire year. Our consciousness needs to be: We are preparing ourselves and the world for what will happen when the night is over—that is, for the end of pain and suffering forever.

The amount of Light that will be received at Shavuot is dependent on each one of us. The amount of energy that will be revealed at the end of the night depends on our excitement, on our connection, on our consciousness. Every one of us is responsible. Every one of us will probably have a completely different level of connection, a completely different experience. But the opportunity for the connection to the Light of the Creator is available to all of us.

CHAPTER 8

Rosh Chodesh
Tammuz

Tammuz is the sign of Cancer, and strong emotions are part of what makes those born under the astrological sign of Cancer unique. Emotions certainly have a positive side, but sometimes in an emotional state we say things we regret, or do things we later wish we hadn't done. All of us who are born in Tammuz, me included, have a special opportunity at this time to truly take control of our emotions because the energy of all emotions originates in this month.

And that is the key point and the key lesson for this month. We need to be in control of our emotions so we can use them in a way that enhances our growth and our connection to the

53

Light of the Creator. So how do we know if we are in control of our emotions?

Well, if we feel joy only when everything is going well, then we are not in control. And in the same way, if we only do things that make us excited or gratify us swiftly, then our actions are not expressions of free choice. We need to ask ourselves how often do we perform acts of sharing that really challenge us, that go beyond what just makes us feel good. As long as emotions control our actions, they will cause disconnection and darkness, and what we feel and what we do will not bring us connection with the Light of the Creator.

Because emotions are tremendously powerful, that energy can be harnessed to assist us in connecting to the Light. To make this clear, I want to discuss three very powerful feelings. They are love, fear, and regret.

According to Kabbalah, the purpose of our spiritual work in this world can be summarized in one single statement: "Love your neighbor as yourself." The starting point for all the fulfillment and blessings that we hope to bring into our lives is dependent on developing our love toward other people. But we need to differentiate between two types of love. On the one hand there is ego love, or selfish love. On the other there is love based on sharing. It is the second kind of love that connects us to the Light, that brings the blessings and fulfillment we all hope for.

When we are involved with people who give us something that we desire whether it is something physical or emotional, we may give love in return for what we have received. But this kind of love is not truly based on sharing. It's a lower level of love. The highest level of love is feeling an innate desire to share with other people *without* getting—or even expecting—anything in return.

A great lesson on this point concerns Abraham the Patriarch. Abraham was the channel for *Chesed,* one of the *Ten Sfirot,* the ten emanations of the Creator's Light that come into this world. The kabbalists teach that *Chesed* is the channel of Right Column energy, of love and kindness. Thus, Abraham's whole life centered around love: His entire purpose was sharing with other people, awakening and growing his love for them. He literally was the channel that opened the gates of love so that it could flow into our world.

Before Abraham, the channel of love from the Supernal World was limited. As a result of Abraham's great work, that channel opened for the world as a whole. Moreover, during the life of Abraham, it was easier for people to share love than at any time before him. But unfortunately, according to the kabbalists, people began using that capability in a negative way until their love was corrupted by selfishness and by ego.

As a result, the Creator had to limit the channel of love again, cutting it back from what it had been in the time of Abraham. This is a very important fact that concerns each of us because we ourselves have the ability to open our own channel of love, and also have the capacity to limit that channel. We open our channel of love by actively awakening and acting on our selfless love towards other people. And the highest level of love is the desire to share with other people who do not give anything in return.

The second emotion I'd like to discuss in relation to Tammuz is fear. *The Zohar,* in the chapter of Noah, has a very interesting discussion on this topic. According to *The Zohar,* when

Noah came out of the ark after the Flood, the Creator told him, "You will be feared by all the animals, and by all of nature. You will have the image of man." *The Zohar* tells us that there are different images, which refer to and depict different levels of connection that govern how we develop ourselves. The ultimate level of development is that of a human being, but we can alter that development and that image, changing and degrading "the image of man" if we perform negative actions.

If our image changes for the worse, the spiritual protection that surrounds us will diminish. Before the generation of the Flood, a wild animal looking up at a human being would see the image of God. All the animals and all of nature had a fear of man. But because of humanity's negative actions, the situation was reversed: Human beings no longer had spiritual protection, and people began fearing animals.

Here *The Zohar* is teaching us a very important lesson. Each of us is born with a *Tzelem Elohim*, an image of God that covers us and shields us from negativity and danger. That protection will stay with us always—unless we ourselves erode it by our own destructive actions or negative consciousness.

The third emotion I'd like to discuss is regret. Many of us have done things that we've regretted, things that hurt us or hurt others. As the kabbalists teach, regret is an important emotion, and it too, has both a positive and a negative side. If we look back at things we've done, become depressed about them and do nothing, that is the negative side of regret. But when our regrets give us a push to do things differently and to change and grow, those regrets connect us to the Light of the Creator.

This brings to mind a story about a kabbalist, Rabbi Abraham Yehoshua Heshil from the town of Apta, also known as the Apta Rebbe. One day, a certain man came to him for a blessing, but when the Apta Rebbe saw him, the Rebbe realized that this man was one of the most evil people alive at that time. So the Apta Rebbe said to this man, "How dare you come into my presence? Leave! I don't want to look at a person as evil as you!"

Of course, the man was shaken by these words. He asked the great kabbalist, "Is there any way for me to correct my soul?"

The Apta Rebbe answered him, "Go away for one year. Don't do anything negative for one year, and meanwhile, find your own way to correct yourself. As you are now, I don't see a way that I can help you."

(As an aside, after the Apta Rebbe met with this man, his children became ill. When the Apta Rebbe saw this, he knew it was because he had shattered a *klippah*, a great shell of negativity surrounding the man. His awakening of the evil man to his own negativity had removed a tremendous amount of darkness from the world, and that negativity was trying to get back at the Apta Rebbe. The point is that it is easy to try to help someone when there's nothing negative that can come of it. A true kabbalist is a person who's willing to help another, regardless of the consequences.)

After his meeting with the Apta Rebbe, the evil man worked diligently for a whole year. In fact, he did as much good as possible, not just for one or two years, but for seven full years. Finally, he came back to the Apta Rebbe, hoping that now the kabbalist would be willing and able to help him.

When he walked into the room, the Apta Rebbe stood up and said, "Who are you? You must be a great soul!"

The man began to weep. He said, "Don't you recognize me? I am that same evil person you saw seven years ago."

The Apta Rebbe saw that the image of God surrounded the man. He saw a tremendous level of connection to the Light. The Apta Rebbe hugged the man and said, "You no longer need anybody like me. Your soul is completely corrected. Not only have you perfected your soul, but you've perfected your body as well. You have achieved complete perfection."

This is a very powerful and significant story because we're talking here about using the emotion of regret as motivation to transform ourselves for the better. The journey toward perfection has to begin with sincere regret for the actions that have brought us to where we are today.

In this month of Tammuz, the month of emotions, we can use love, fear, and regret to achieve the purpose for which we came to this world—to attain a true and complete connection to the Light of the Creator that will bring us ultimate joy and fulfillment forever.

CHAPTER 9

Rosh Chodesh Av

Av (Leo) is a unique month in that the energy of the first half of Av is very different from that of the second half. The first half of this month is considered to be heavy, dark, and generally negative. But the second half of Av is the most positive of all the months. In fact, the fifteenth day of this month, Tu B'Av, called the Day of Love by the kabbalists, begins one of the highest levels of connection of any time of the year. But we also know that the ninth day of Av, called Tisha B'Av, is the most negative day of the year; the destruction of the first and the second Temples occurred on this day in history. So there's a unique dichotomy in this month: The first half is very negative, while the second half is very positive.

The kabbalists teach that the Tetragrammaton—*Yud, Hei, Vav,* and *Hei*—the four-letter name of God, is really a channel through which the Light of the Creator flows into our world. Different permutations of the Tetragrammaton signify different types of energy, and each month has a very specialized and unique Tetragrammaton combination of letters. Before we can understand and connect with the energy of any month, we need to know the Tetragrammaton combination that draws and reveals Light into that month.

Looking at this month's combination—*Hei, Vav, Yud* and *Hei*—we get an understanding of Av's basic duality. We can see the first two letters, *Hei* and *Vav*, have reversed their usual positions, so that the last letter of the Tetragrammaton (*Hei*) is now first and the third letter of the Tetragrammaton (*Vav*) is now second. The last two letters of this combination, *Yud* and *Hei*, are in their usual order. We know that these last two letters are numerically equal to fifteen, with the *Yud* being ten and the *Hei* being five. So the last two letters signify the last fifteen days of the month.

We will want to meditate on this Tetragrammaton combination whenever we need an injection of Light during the month of Av—and certainly at the beginning of the month, there may be many of these opportunities. So remember these four letters and their combination. These are channels by which we draw Light into this month, not only for ourselves but for the world.

The concept of a difficult beginning and a positive ending actually permeates all of our lives. The kabbalists teach that to reach the Light, to gain the fulfillment we seek and the blessings we desire, we have to go through a difficult process of transformation: We have to change our *Desire to Receive for the Self Alone* into a *Desire to Share.* That process is never easy, but it's important to understand that the beginning is the most difficult part. And as we have seen, this difficulty brings its own reward: The beginning of the month of Av which includes the most negative day of the year, Tisha B'Av, brings us towards Tu B'Av, one of the highest connections of the year.

We've discussed the kabbalist metaphor of the *klippah*, or shell of negativity or darkness that covers every potential Light. Before any revelation of Light, the *klippah* must come off. In the context of this month we see that the ups and downs of life are essentially two sides of the same coin, but the underlying positive nature of a seemingly negative situation may be hidden by the *klippah*. One of the first lessons of this month is not to withdraw from difficult situations, but to realize that within the darkness, within the shell, there is great Light. Darkness is there only so we can find the hidden spark of Light.

A second crucial concept this month is the idea of feeling the pain of the world—or, as the kabbalists say, feeling the pain of the *Shechinah*, which is the feminine aspect of the Light of the Creator that manifests in this world. When we think about feeling the pain of others, we may tell ourselves that it's an altruistic thing to do, or a sharing action that we can take if we have the time. But most of us don't have the time. We are too busy at work or with our families. Who has the time, or the stomach, to go out and uncover the pain of others and not just to find it, but to actually feel that pain?

But consider what the Bible says about Moses while he was growing up in Egypt. He would go out every single day and see—and feel—the pain of the Israelites who were enslaved by the Egyptians. The kabbalists teach that it was that willingness to feel another's pain that brought the great connection that Moses developed with the Creator.

In *The Gift of the Bible*, Rav Ashlag speaks about this idea. He says that as long as we are comfortable with our *Desire to Receive for the Self Alone* and consistently involved with our selfish concerns, it is almost impossible to truly feel the pain around us. As a result, it is also impossible to truly share with others. Rav Ashlag says that only by continuously working toward removing the *Desire to Receive for the Self Alone* can we hope to begin to feel the pain of others.

Again, remember that the reason we want to make empathy a consistent part of our spiritual work is not simply because we want to share. Rather, it is the knowledge that we cannot truly bring the blessings and fulfillment of the Light into every area of our lives unless we make feeling the pain of others an integral part of our spiritual work. Rav Ashlag refers to the Talmud on this subject: Only a person who assumes part of the pain of the world can generate enough merit to partake of the ultimate joy. We cannot have one without the other. If we divorce ourselves from the pain of the world, then we also divorce ourselves from the Light of the Creator.

Just as we need to have consciousness of connection with other people at Rosh Chodesh, we need also to make our connection to *Sefer Yetzirah, The Book of Formation*, written by Abraham the Patriarch. Every time we connect to the writings and the teachings of the great kabbalists, we do so because we want to draw their wisdom. But even more importantly, we want to connect to their consciousness and to their Light. Through *The Book of Formation*, we not only draw the wisdom and the Light that Abraham the Patriarch put there but we also connect ourselves to the consciousness and the Light of Abraham.

Abraham, in *The Book of Formation*, reveals the letters that are the channels for the energies of this month. He writes: "The

Creator took the letter *Tet*, and through the power of the letter *Tet* created the sign of Leo in the month of Av." This means
that all the Light that we hope to draw in this month, all the
fulfillment and all the blessings that we want to draw in this
month, will come to us through the letter *Tet*.

Just as we learned earlier about the Tetragrammaton combination for Av, we now also know the individual Hebrew letter
that is associated with this month. As always, it's important to
keep reminding ourselves that Hebrew letters are powerful
forms of energy. They were created so that we can draw Light
into our lives. So any time throughout this month when we
want to draw additional Light; when we find ourselves in trying situations, we can meditate on this letter. *Tet* is the letter
that is the channel for the abundance of Light that is available
in this month.

Abraham also explains that specific physical powers can also be
heightened during a particular month. The month of
Tammuz, for example, connects us to the power of sight. Now,
in this month of Av, we are connected to the power of hearing.
What exactly does this mean?

Most of us are born with the ability to hear, at least on the
physical level. But there is also a more important and a higher
level of hearing—a level we can call "spiritual hearing." The
kabbalists continually remind us that beyond the world that
we experience every day there is a higher reality that influences
our lives. Unfortunately, many of us are not aware of this higher reality, but its influence is certainly more powerful than the
influence of our physical surroundings.

So just as there is physical sight, there is also spiritual sight.
Just as there is physical hearing, there is spiritual hearing. The

kabbalists explain that every day voices go out, voices that can be heard by those that are truly connected to the Light. Who among us would not want to hear these voices and the messages they bring? Who among us would not want to have that power to hear? Often we wish we could get answers to our questions, and we wish there was a power that could tell us what to do. Wouldn't it be wonderful if each of us had the ability to hear a guiding voice for each of the hundreds of decisions we need to make in our lives?

Most of us have difficulty in truly hearing such messages because we have caused damage to our "spiritual ears." There are many ways we may have done that. When we listen to somebody talk negatively about somebody else, we are damaging our spiritual hearing. When we hear things that are not of a positive nature, we injure our spiritual ears. As a result, if we are supposed to get a spiritual message today, a very clear internal message that requires the power of spiritual hearing, that message may be unavailable to us.

Once again, the messages that I'm referring to are not spoken with a physical voice. These are internal, spiritual messages that require the power of spiritual hearing. We inherently have the ability and gift to receive these messages and this guidance. But if today I hear somebody speak negatively about somebody else and I let it go—or maybe even enjoy it and laugh about it—I have done damage to my spiritual hearing. The message that was supposed to come to me so clearly either won't be heard by me at all or will not be clear.

We need to recognize the relationship between the damage that we do to our spiritual hearing (the Cause) and the damage that brings into our lives (the Effect). When our spiritual hearing is damaged, when we don't hear the messages intended for us, then we lack clarity about the decisions that we are called upon to make in our lives. This is where the letter *Tet* can be of help. Through the letter *Tet* in the month of Av, we can reconnect to the power of true hearing and remove the barriers that we ourselves have created. Again, how wonderful it will be for every single one of us when our spiritual hearing is restored.

We always need to remember that the Creator does not leave us here in this world without direction. The direction is clear, but we put up barriers that obscure that direction and make invisible the path that is set so perfectly for us. We cannot see and we cannot hear, and therefore we cannot follow the correct path. So in this month, we need to meditate on the letter *Tet* to restore our spiritual hearing, and in an even larger sense, we must also make a decision never to damage our spiritual hearing.

When we begin to study Kabbalah, we often try to stay away from complex ideas, yet, understanding the month of Av does require some thought. But the lessons of this month are so important that I hope we can learn from them and take their messages to heart.

The essence of Av is based upon the kabbalistic teaching that there are two aspects to the Light of the Creator. The male aspect is referred to as *Zeir Anpin*, and the female aspect as *Malchut*. Sometimes in *The Zohar*, the first aspect is referred to as the Holy One, Blessed be He, and the second is referred to as the *Shechinah*, the Light that protects us as our Spiritual Mother. When we perform a positive action—when we share or when we resist anger—we create a degree of union between these two aspects, a coming together of the Supernal Male and Female, which reveals Light. The greater and more difficult our action, the greater the union that will come about.

When we create unity between the Supernal Male and Female, all the fulfillment that we desire, need, and are destined to have, becomes available to us. But this also holds true on the negative side. Our negative actions create disunity and separation between the Supernal Male and Female. When there is this separation, no Light flows into our world, and there is pain and suffering. This is why there is so much suffering in the world today. When they do unite, and the degree to which they unite, brings Light and blessings and fulfillment.

Whenever we perform an act of selfless sharing, an action that reveals Light, an action that seems difficult or even impossible, we are preparing the great union of *Zeir Anpin* and *Malchut*. We are preparing our world for the time when pain and suffering can end. As *The Zohar* says, "Together we will prepare our world for the great union. Whoever takes part in this preparation will be protected from above and below, and will have protection throughout the entire year." As Rav Ashlag explains, bringing about the union of *Zeir Anpin* and *Malchut* is the true purpose of *The Zohar*, just as it is also the true purpose of our lives.

So now that we understand the concept of the Supernal Union, we can come back to our month of Av. This is a month of separation—at least during the first half—and it is a month in which we must feel the pain that this separation brings. The kabbalists teach that without developing our ability to feel the pain of others, we cannot completely connect to the Light. Today and every day, as long as there is pain and suffering, the female aspect of the Light, the *Shechinah*, is in pain. She is in pain for every person who's dying, for every person who's starving, for every child who doesn't have parents. Every aspect of pain in our world is felt by the Creator, and if we want to receive the Light of the Creator, we have to be like the Creator.

One of the most important ways we can do this is through our feeling of pain for other people throughout the world.

One of the beautiful things about Kabbalah is that it explains not only the spiritual laws themselves but also how they influence us in our everyday lives. Rather than simply understanding the need to feel the pain of others as a purely spiritual concept, we realize that this is how we connect to the Light of the Creator. So in this month, unlike any other month, the unique principle we need to work on is feeling the pain of others. *The Zohar* teaches that feeling the pain of the *Shechinah*—feeling the pain that the Creator feels for the suffering in our world—will bring us to greatness.

Once, a great kabbalist was approached by one of his students whose son was terribly ill. The doctors had given up all hope. The student thought, "If anybody can help now, maybe it's my teacher."

So the student asked the great kabbalist, "Is there anything you can do? Can you pray? Can you open the Gates of Heaven?" So the kabbalist prayed. But after a while he turned to his student and said, "I'm sorry. There's nothing that I can do. The Gates of Heaven are closed."

Of course, the student was heartbroken. He got on his horse and traveled back toward his home. But after riding for five or ten minutes, he heard somebody galloping after him at full speed. Seeing that it was his teacher, he stopped by the side of the road. As soon as the great kabbalist caught up with him, the student asked, "Were you able to open the Gates of Heaven?"

The teacher said, "No, I'm sorry to tell you again that the Gates of Heaven are closed. But I realized after you left that if

I can't help your son, the least I can do is cry with you." And they sat down by the side of the road and they cried together.

The story goes on to show how the two men were able to find a way to save the student's son, but that's not the important point. The key teaching of the story is that there is always something more that we can do. And one thing we can always do is feel the pain of others. This story tells us that no matter how much we think we've done, there is always something more that we can do. If we can't help somebody, we can cry with them. We can feel their pain.

None of us have come even close to our full potential for helping. It is the special call of this month to work on that. We need to find all the ways that we can help. And when we think we've found all the ways, we can remember this story. There is *always* something else we can do.

CHAPTER 10

Rosh Chodesh Elul

To understand the energy of this month, it is best to start with its Tetragrammaton combination of letters. For this month of Elul, the combination of letters is *Hei*, *Hei*, *Vav*, and *Yud*. It's interesting that the first two letters of the combination (*Hei* in both cases) signify the female aspect of the Tetragrammaton. The first *Hei* corresponds to the *Sfirah* of *Binah*, and the second *Hei* to the *Sfirah* of *Malchut*. The last two letters, the *Vav* and the *Yud*, relate to the male aspect.

The kabbalists teach that the month of Elul, with its sign of Virgo, has the unique power to cleanse negativity. We live in the dimension of *Malchut*, which is the physical world. This is the world in which we make mistakes, and in which we create barriers between ourselves and the Light of the Creator. Every time we are responsible for an action that is not positive—if we hurt someone else or if we hurt ourselves, if we speak negatively about another person, or if we commit an act that we know in some way or another is going to hurt somebody else—that act creates negative energy. As the Rav says, "We can say we're sorry, but apologizing doesn't remove the negative energy."

How then can we remove that negative energy? How do we wipe the slate of all the negative actions we've committed this year, or even before this year? Even more importantly, how can we take that negativity and transform it into Light?

This is a great opportunity. The kabbalists tell us that if a person who has performed a negative act is able to transform that energy, he's even better off than he was before committing the negative act. In other words, if a person who has done tremendously negative actions transforms all that energy back into Light, he generates more Light than someone who has never done anything negative. This is an amazing teaching, but how does this process of transformation work?

When we have committed a negative action, that negative energy stays with us until we cleanse it. If we don't cleanse it in this incarnation, the negative energy will carry over into our next lifetime. Kabbalistically, the process of cleansing negativity and transforming it into Light means taking the darkness of *Malchut*, the physical world, and elevating it into the much higher dimension of *Binah*, which the kabbalists call the Supernal Mother. The power to do that is the great gift of this month.

How can we partake of this gift? What must we do in order to elevate darkness and transform it into Light?

The kabbalists tell us that the first and most important step is to acknowledge our own negativity. The only way to turn negative actions into Light is by bringing them clearly to the forefront of our consciousness. Any action that we forget or exclude cannot be transformed. Therefore, one of the most important things we need to do this month is simply *remember*.

The kabbalists also say that the most destructive effect of Adam's sin was blinding us to our own darkness, to our own negative acts. When we have a thought such as, "I spoke badly about that person, but he really deserved it," the root of this thought is Adam's sin. And the worst part is that we are unable to transform that negativity into Light because we haven't brought the negativity clearly into our consciousness. To whatever degree we understand and are clear about how negative we have been, the negativity will be cleansed. To the degree that we remain blind to our negative actions, the darkness of those actions will not be transformed into Light.

During the month of Elul, the gift of elevation from *Malchut* to *Binah*, of transformation of all our negative actions into Light, is much too valuable to miss. By awakening all our past negativity in this month, we will transform it.

The importance of this month extends back to before the creation of the world. According to the teachings of Kabbalah, the physical world was actually created in the month of Tishrei, which follows Elul. Rosh Hashanah, the first two days of Tishrei, marked the creation of the physical world. But—and this is one of the most beautiful teachings of Kabbalah—even before the creation of the world, there was the Thought of Creation that occurred in the month of Elul.

In the physical world, before we can build a house we must envision the house in our mind. Then we draw up plans. After the plans are approved, we can start building. This entire process takes time, and after a month or two of work, we still can't expect to see a perfectly finished house. In much the same way, the month of Elul, which precedes the creation of this world in Tishrei, is the time of the Thought of Creation. In this Thought lies the perfection of the world—and the perfection of every single one of its people.

No matter where we find ourselves in our spiritual work, this month allows us to tap into our true perfection. This is the perfection that is ordained for each of us, no matter how many lifetimes it may take us to reach that point. The perfection of the Thought of Creation never dissipates. It is always there for us to access, and this is never truer than during this month of Elul. Also available is the ultimate fulfilment, the ultimate removal of all pain and suffering from the world.

We need to remember that no matter how much negativity we have created, no matter how deep we go into darkness, our soul—our essence, our seed—never becomes impure. It never becomes dark. What this month offers us is the ability to reconnect to the part of us that is pure and new, that is completely of the Light and free from darkness.

Abraham the Patriarch, in *Sefer Yetzirah, The Book of Formation*, tells us that the letter *Yud* created Elul, with its sign of Virgo, because *Yud* signifies the energy that never gets dark or defiled. It is that aspect of us that is pure and new. Abraham explains that our essence always remains that of the *Yud*. No matter how much negativity we've created, our essence remains pure. One of the things that the Negative Side tries to use against us is the idea that we've done so much wrong that we can't possibly correct it. Don't listen to the Negative Side. Every one of us has the *Yud* within.

We need to understand the extraordinary gift of this month, the gift of going back to our true selves before any negativity was attached. This awakens within us the original Source of our soul, and we can do that, even when the Negative Side tells us we can't. If we consciously know that we can remove all that negativity, no matter what we've done previously, then we can connect back to our perfection, our true essence.

Another valuable idea in *The Book of Formation* is that the power of Elul can only be manifested through action. Consciousness first, followed by action, because without action the gifts of Elul can pass us by.

So remember these three lessons. The first lesson is to actively engage in the elevation of all negativity for the purpose of transforming it into Light. The second lesson is to awaken our understanding that our true perfection, the *Yud* that every single one of us has within us can never be damaged. And the third lesson is to tap into and manifest that ultimate perfection both for ourselves and for the world.

Another secret revealed by the kabbalists is that we can understand the energy of words by their acronyms. The word *Elul* (*Alef, Lamed, Vav, Lamed*) is an acronym for the term *ani ledodi vedodi li*, based on verse 6:3 in Song of Songs written by King Solomon: "I am to my beloved, and my beloved is towards me."

This verse refers to *DESIRE*. In this month we can awaken desire for what we really need on both the physical and the spiritual levels. Both Rav Isaac Luria, who lived more than 400 years ago, and Rav Yehuda Brandwein, the Rav's teacher and one of twentieth century's greatest kabbalists, taught the importance of awakening true desire for the Light *before* the month of Tishrei, the month that follows Elul. So in the month we must ask that this desire become awakened.

There is a fundamental lesson here, one that we often forget. The only way to draw Light is to have a Vessel, and the only Vessel is *desire*. To the degree that we awaken true desire, Light will be revealed. Desire is the Vessel for the Light we need to draw for the entire year to come.

If a person does not do the work of awakening desire in this month of Elul, it will be very difficult to manifest the desired Light on Rosh Hashanah and in the month of Tishrei as well as during the year to come. So what we do now is the first and most significant step towards ensuring blessings in both the physical sense and the spiritual sense.

There is a story in the book of 2 Kings 4:1-6 that begins with a woman, the wife of a prophet, calling out to Elisha, one of the greatest of all the prophets. She says, "My husband, one of the prophets, has passed away. And because we are left with so many debts, one of the creditors wants to take away my children to be servants."

So Elisha says to this woman, "Tell me what you have in your house."

She replies, "I have nothing left in my house except a small jar of oil."

Then the prophet Elisha tells her, "Go to all of your neighbors and gather all the cups and bowls and pans that you can find in their houses. Once you've gathered all these vessels, bring them into your house, close the door behind yourself and your children, and you'll be able to fill up all those vessels. Just pour the oil from your small jar into all of those vessels."

She does as he told her. She collected the vessels from her neighbors' homes, and then returned to her house and closed the door behind herself and her children. She took her one small jar and began to pour out the oil and just kept pouring.

Then she said to her son, "Bring some more vessels." But when her son replied that there were no more vessels, the oil stopped flowing.

We can draw a clear understanding from this story. As long as there were more vessels to be filled, the flow was endless. Once there were no more vessels, the flow stopped. So when we talk about the importance of awakening a desire in this month, we have to be very clear about what this means. We have to be *full of desire* during the month of Elul. In fact, the degree to which we may think we have desire is not even close to the true desire that we should have. Because of this, we limit the amount of Light we receive.

When we speak about desire, we need to differentiate between two different forms. There is the *Desire to Receive for the Self Alone*: "I want more of this or more of that to make my ego more fulfilled." This, obviously, is not the desire we need to awaken during Elul; on the contrary, we want to diminish those desires. Instead, we need to kindle the desire that is based on the *Desire to Receive for the Sake of Sharing*. This means we can ask for everything in this month, but we have to be very clear about *why* we desire it. If I desire something to fulfil my ego needs, that will not draw and reveal Light for the coming year. But if my Desire is to Receive for the Sake of Sharing, that is a true Vessel into which the Light of the Creator can flow. Yes, we can want more money. Yes, we can want more power. But why do we want it? This needs to be clear in our minds. If we want something because we want to share more of what we receive, then the flow will be endless.

The kabbalists teach us that in order to awaken a true Vessel, in order to awaken a true desire, we have to quiet the ego. As long as our selfish desire is making noise, we will be without a true Vessel. To truly build the Vessel that achieves the purpose of this month—a limitless, endless Vessel for the coming year—we need to quiet the *Desire to Receive for the Self Alone* and to awaken a true *Desire to Receive for the Sake of Sharing.* And in the month of Elul, we need to awaken our desire for everything *right now.*

We have learned three things about creating a Vessel this month. The first is that we have to awaken limitless desire. Secondly, we have to purify our desire, which takes time and effort. And finally, to complete the process of creating the Vessel, we have to develop certainty and urgency. We have to say, "In this month, I want to ask for everything, both for my own purpose and for the purpose of the world. My life depends on it, and I want it now and I can have it now."

When we do that during Elul, whatever blessings we might hope for on Rosh Hashanah will manifest even more fully than anything we might ever hope for or imagine.

CHAPTER 11

Rosh Chodesh Tishrei

According to the kabbalists, Tishrei (Libra) is the first month of the year. We know that there are many different cosmic spiritual connections—commonly called holidays—throughout this month. So we need to understand the power of these connections and how to best use them.

The *Zohar* explains that the first day of Tishrei is Rosh Hashanah, or the beginning of the year. Historically, this is the time of Creation. Every year at Rosh Hashanah, we go back to the moment when Adam was created. In other words, we have the ability to connect to the same energy that Adam connected with at the moment he came into being.

The unique configuration of the Tetragrammaton—the four Hebrew letters that spell out the name of God—for Tishrei is *Vav, Hei, Yud,* and *Hei,* which actually spells out the word *vahiyeh,* meaning "and it will be." This refers to the future, and is our first clue of the importance and the gift of this month. This is the time when we lay the groundwork and create the foundation for the type of Light and life we are going to have in the coming year. Clearly, this is very important, so our spiritual work and our consciousness need to be very strong and focused.

We will use this tool not only on Rosh Chodesh but throughout the month to draw the Light of rejuvenation, the Light of complete renewal, the Light of completely new beginnings. We don't want this year to be just another version of the year before. We want this year to be even greater than the year before, greater than any year we've ever had. In this month, and especially in the first two days of this month, we want to draw not just more Light, not just greater Light, but Light that will transform every aspect of our lives, both spiritually and physically. As *The Zohar* explains, without consciousness and awareness on our part, the Light of the Creator cannot manifest. We need to desire and ask for complete renewal. It isn't enough simply to know that this gift is available. We need to access and use the tool of this month, through the Tetragrammaton combination, to draw down a completely new Light of renewal and rejuvenation.

Kabbalists tell us that every year that is poor in the beginning is wealthy at the end. What they mean is that as we come to the beginning of the year in Tishrei, we need to create a consciousness of having nothing and wanting everything. We need to feel that we have nothing as the year begins. Then we need to ask for *everything*—health, sustenance, blessings, and complete fulfillment. We also should understand that we do not have anything—that nothing remains—of the previous year, and we are asking for everything, knowing that we will receive it all.

A very beautiful story of the Baal Shem Tov relates to this. Often the Baal Shem Tov would travel with his students from city to city, assisting people and praying or meditating with them. Very often he would let his horses take him wherever they wanted. He would ask his driver, Alexei, to literally turn away from the horses and let them lead him where he had to go.

Once the Baal Shem Tov gathered his students together and said, "I have received a message from above that I have to go to a certain town. Please join me in this journey." So they got in the carriage and traveled a great distance until the horses stopped outside a little shack. The Baal Shem Tov knocked on the door, and when a man and his wife opened it, the Baal Shem Tov spoke in a demanding voice that was very unusual for him. He said, "I'm hungry and I want food. We've traveled a long way. Do you have anything for us to eat?"

These people were obviously not very wealthy and they did not have a great deal of food. But they knew of the Baal Shem Tov. They wanted to give him whatever he wanted. So they opened all the cupboards and took whatever they had and put it on the table. As the Baal Shem Tov ate, all the students were embarrassed because the Baal Shem Tov was eating as if he had never eaten before in his life. He finished all the food in the house. There was literally nothing left.

But that was not the end. The Baal Shem Tov turned to the man and his wife and said, "Is there anything else to eat? I'm still hungry!"

The husband and wife went into the kitchen to confer. They were not sure what to do. They did have one cow, but their cow was the only thing that sustained them; they sold the cow's milk, which was their only income. They thought, "This cow is our livelihood, but this great kabbalistic master says he's still hungry. Maybe we should let him eat the cow."

So they slaughtered the cow and prepared the meat for the Baal Shem Tov. He ate it greedily. He ate the entire cow, leaving the man and his wife with nothing. Then he thanked them for the meal, got back in his carriage, and drove away with his students. For their part, the students didn't ask for an explanation of what had happened because they knew that their master always had reasons for what he did.

Many years later, the Baal Shem Tov was walking in a village with his students. A beautiful carriage passed by. Just then the man in the carriage saw the Baal Shem Tov. He ordered the carriage to stop and he stepped out. As he approached the Baal Shem Tov, he said, "Thank you! Thank you! Because of you, I am where I am today. After you left me with nothing, I went into the forest and began to pray. I asked the Creator, 'What am I going to do now? I have no way to feed my family.' And as I was walking in the forest, praying and crying, I stumbled over something on the ground. I saw it was a box, and when I opened the box, I found gold coins inside! Of course, I was overjoyed. I took the money home, began to invest it, and soon became a very wealthy man."

Then the Baal Shem Tov turned to his students and said, "This man and his wife were destined for riches, but they were settling only for what they already had. Every day they would get a little money for the cow's milk, but they never received any of their much greater blessings because they never asked for them. They were satisfied. They *settled* for what they had. They had lowered their expectations and because they never asked for anything, they didn't receive anything. So I had to take away what they *had* in order for them to receive what they *deserved.* Only when this man and his wife had nothing, when they could no longer just settle, did they begin to ask for everything, opening the door to the true riches they had always been destined to have."

This is a lesson for all of us. Every single one of us is destined for greatness, but because we settle for less, we don't fulfill our destiny. We settle physically and we settle spiritually. But in the month of Tishrei we cannot settle: We don't want this to be a year in which we receive anything less than what we are truly destined to have. Therefore, we have to begin this month with a mindset of poverty, with the understanding that we have nothing and we want everything. A year that begins with the consciousness of poverty can end, as the kabbalists teach, with both physical and spiritual wealth.

The second very important lesson is that we should not settle for anything less nor be satisfied with what we have. And the third lesson is that we need to have total certainty in our destiny, and then act in accordance with that certainty.

It's interesting that for many people the first two days of Tishrei are often very intense days and a time without joy. These are days in which people pray, make spiritual connections, and meditate with the knowledge that they are building the foundation for the whole year to come. But the Baal Shem Tov taught that there should be joy in everything, even in the first two days of Tishrei on Rosh Hashanah. When others were sad and serious, for the Baal Shem Tov and his students there was singing and dancing.

This is a key point because *The Zohar* teaches that it is our consciousness that draws the Light of the Creator. If we begin this year with uncertainty, doubtful of what lies ahead, that's the type of year that we will draw: a year of uncertainty and deprivation. We have to remember that we want to draw the Light of rejuvenation and that nothing from the previous year belongs to us; there are no holdovers or leftovers. We want everything, and we want it new.

And to have a positive outcome in every endeavor we begin during the new year, we need to consciously draw the Light of the Creator into that undertaking. When we wake up in the morning, our first thought needs to be: "I want the Light of the Creator to permeate this entire day." Now, at the beginning of the year, we have to consciously say, "I want the Light of the Creator to fill every aspect of my life and to permeate everything that I'm going to do in this coming year."

To understand this, Rav Ashlag explains how when *The Zohar* describes the great kabbalists traveling from one place to another, the sages weren't physically traveling; rather they were going from one spiritual level of consciousness to another. A passage in *The Zohar* puts it this way: "Rav Shimon was traveling with his son, Rav Elazar, and two other great kabbalists, Rav Yosi and Rav Chiya. As they were traveling, Rav Elazar said to his father, 'In order for this path to reveal Light for us, we need to have you say some words of wisdom and to reveal some secrets.' Then Rav Shimon began, 'When a person wants to begin a new path and he wants to be sure the Light of the Creator is manifest there, before he starts on the path he should consciously ask the Light of the Creator to become part of this travel. But if a person does not consciously and specifically ask the Light to manifest in this path, then the Light of the Creator will not come.'"

Here Rav Shimon is showing us that we have to consciously ask the Light to enter into the new path or direction we wish to take. If we don't do that, we can endeavor to make connections, but the Light will not come. Therefore when Rav Shimon bar Yochai was traveling with his son and the two other kabbalists, they of course, had a powerful connection to the Light, but they knew that if they wanted to truly bring the Light of the Creator into this new path they were following, then they had to consciously ask for it.

This teaching holds true throughout the incoming new year. In fact, it's true for everything that we begin. We have to be sure that we're consciously asking for the Light to enter every aspect of our new endeavor. Certainly in this month of Tishrei as we prepare the year to come, we have to make sure that we have this constant consciousness of asking the Creator, "Please come into my life. Come into this month. Come into my entire year."

So remember and use these four levels of consciousness:

1) Meditate on the Tetragrammaton combination: *Vav*, *Hei*, *Yud*, and *Hei*. This is good for creating the future, creating the first level of consciousness, and for rejuvenation, knowing that everything from last year remains part of last year and does not roll over into the new year. We must tell ourselves: "I want everything to be new in this year. I want my physical self to be new. I want my spiritual self to be new. I want my connection to the Light to be brand new, like the first time."

2) The second level of consciousness that we need to keep in our minds, certainly on the first two days of this month but also throughout this month, is the idea of poverty. We come into this month knowing that we have nothing. We're not

settling for anything that we have had until now. We want everything new, and we want everything greater than before. We want to achieve the greatness for which we came to this world, and we will no longer *settle* for what we have, both in the physical and in the spiritual sense.

3) The third very important consciousness of this month is having certainty and having joy in that certainty. You and I know that we are going to draw into this month all the Light that we need so that the year we will have will be the year that we want—a year filled with endless blessings and Light, with certainty and joy in that certainty.

4) In the fourth level, which is important throughout the year but so much more so in this month, we need to consciously ask for the Light of the Creator to permeate this entire month. We must ask again and again and again, because as Rav Shimon bar Yochai revealed to us in *The Zohar*, it is only by consciously and specifically asking for the Light of the Creator to come into our month and thereby into the year that the Light of the Creator will come.

By incorporating these four levels of consciousness into the first two days of the month of Tishrei, as well as during the rest of the month, we will be able to truly draw into our lives the year that we want, a year filled with blessings, with fulfillment, and with endless Light.

CHAPTER 12

Rosh Hashanah

Rosh Hashanah is the beginning of the year, so of course it's a time when we are preparing for and looking forward to what will happen in the coming months. But Rosh Hashanah is also a time when we return to the purity of the first beginning. As the kabbalists tell us, no matter how many negative actions we have committed, our true, original essence—the spark of the Creator's Light that lies within us—never becomes diminished or disconnected. At Rosh Hashanah we reconnect both to our origin as individuals and also to the origin of all humankind. We are literally born anew.

Kabbalah teaches that every one of us was present before the sin of Adam. We were all there at the Creator's Thought of Creation and at the moment when the perfection of that Thought was manifested. We always have perfection within us, and in the two days of Rosh Hashanah we can reconnect to it. To set up the coming year perfectly, we have to regain access to that part of ourselves that is perfect. This is the perfection that existed before the sin of Adam when the world was free from darkness and chaos.

It's important to understand that this is both an individual and a collective process. It transcends our individual identities, and it extends beyond our physical location in the world. The Rav always made it very clear that if you are in a certain location making your connection to the Light, the effect of the Light that is revealed through you cannot be restricted by physical boundaries. From your location, you are creating a source of Light. You are performing a great service not only for yourself, but for the city you are in and even for the world. Light is not contained by walls or borders.

The Rav always stressed this concept, and at Rosh Hashanah we need to keep it in mind. Wherever we are we reveal Light and this in turn inspires others to share far beyond what we can perceive through our physical senses. Inspiring people to share with others is the greatest possible accomplishment. If we inspire one person who then inspires ten people or fifty people, so much more Light is revealed. When we receive wisdom, we cannot hold it for ourselves. In fact, this is how we know that a person has gained wisdom: They have a true *Desire to Share*. Nothing draws blessings more than desire. For me, it's a tremendous gift to see people inspired to share the Light with others. That sharing is the process by which we are taking steps, one after the other, to end pain and suffering in this world.

Let's be very clear about what this means. At Rosh Hashanah we make the decision to connect back to the absolute perfection that we all have within our souls and to share the Light of that connection. We are not choosing just to be a *little bit better* than we were last year. Rosh Hashanah is an opportunity for *complete and true transformation.* It is a time for saying: "I cannot accept the place that I'm in. I can't be comfortable with the person that I am. Once and for all, I reject my ego and the *Desire to Receive for the Self Alone.* I must completely change— and I will."

We have to know that we have nothing at the present moment but that now we are going to have everything. We are going to choose LIFE. We are going to ask the Creator for the power and the consciousness in the coming year to become completely dedicated to the *Desire to Share.* By making this decision during the two days of Rosh Hashanah, we inscribe ourselves in the Book of Life.

You may doubt that you have the ability to make such a profound change, and based on what has happened so far in your life, that doubt may seem well founded. But many stories in *The Zohar* and the Talmud tell of individuals who did not begin their lives as people of sharing. These people encountered events that awakened in them not only the need to better themselves but also the need to completely and fundamentally change who they were.

Often, we come to moments when we doubt whether we deserve blessings or abundance in our lives. That doubt comes from the Negative Side. The reality beyond that doubt is this: Our true essence, our soul, that spark of the Creator's Light within us is consistently connected to the Creator. We can cover it up with veils of darkness, but that spark never becomes disconnected; it never becomes diminished.

Along with doubt, another of our negative qualities as human beings is the ability to settle. We find ourselves in a difficult situation, and we get used to it. We set limits on how much change is really possible. This is like re-arranging the deck chairs on the Titanic. The boat is sinking, but we try to make the chairs look nicer. Almost always, when we think about spiritual transformation, we settle for a fraction of what we could become. We pick five percent of our lives and wonder how we can improve that tiny portion. The reality is, we have *unlimited potential* so we should not be comfortable with anything but *unlimited results.*

According to a famous kabbalistic teaching, in the nine months prior to our birth, every one of us is taught all the secrets of the universe by a certain angel. We see everything that we can learn and do and become. Then when we come into this world, we are made to forget everything that we have learned. But if we are going to forget the wisdom, what was the purpose of teaching it to us in the first place?

Kabbalists explain that in the true essence of our soul, we never forget what we have been taught. The wisdom is always there; our task is to bring it into our consciousness. Rosh Hashanah is an opportunity to do that. We are not just studying or blowing the *shofar.* We are strengthening our consciousness and sending our awareness out to the rest of the world. On Rosh Hashanah, *The Zohar* tells us, the true essence of the Light of *Binah* is awakened by the blowing of the *shofar.* Now we can share this awakening with the world as a whole.

We know that the writings of Rav Ashlag are not simply teachings. By reading his words we are actually connecting to his essence. In one of the footnotes to his work, Rav Ashlag discusses the importance of spreading the wisdom of Kabbalah. He writes: "Why is our generation ready, unlike any other? I feel in my entire being, in all of my body, that all of the promises in *The Zohar* concerning the revelation of this wisdom at the End of Days, even to the youngest of people, were intended for our generation. That is why I took it upon myself to explain the writings from the Ari, about the Tree of Life, and to reveal these secrets to the world. It is because I feel in my entire being that now is the time for these secrets to be revealed to the entire world."

Rav Ashlag says this revelation has nothing to do with him. It is because of the readiness of the generation in which he finds himself. Those who were chosen to make great revelations throughout history—Moses, Rav Shimon bar Yochai, Rav Isaac Luria (the Ari)—all functioned at a very high spiritual level, but the readiness of their generation was even more important.

That's why Rav Ashlag's soul was sent here at a particular moment in history and why we are the beneficiaries of his presence. Every day we should thank the Creator for allowing us to be born into a generation that is ready for this great revelation.

We know that we do not connect to *The Zohar* simply to gain understanding. As we have discussed, the words of *The Zohar* awaken our connection to the Tree of Life. There is no other day of the year when this is as important as it is at Rosh Hashanah. We want to plant the seed on this day so that all of our year ahead is connected to *Etz Chaim*, the Tree of Life.

The Zohar states that Rosh Hashanah is a day when the Creator, the King, sits on the Throne of Judgment. Then the Negative Side comes and blocks the door to the King and demands judgment. But the Creator has given us the secret of blowing the *shofar* to awaken mercy from below to above. *The Zohar* says that the sound emanating from the *shofar* brings together the three columns—Right, Left, and Central, representing fire, water, and air—in the singular voice and the Supernal Voice, which is *Binah*. In this way the ultimate perfection of life is awakened and all the judgment that the Negative Side tried to arouse becomes confused and is sent away.

Moreover, at Rosh Hashanah we read the Torah story of the Binding of Isaac. As *The Zohar* makes clear, Abraham faced ten tests in his life, ten moments in which he moved to a higher spiritual level. The Binding of Isaac was Abraham's final test. Before connecting to the Light in a deeper and stronger way, we too, must each go through a test, something that is contrary to our nature. It is at these moments that we have an opportunity to truly fulfill our potential. I hope every one of us desires in the year to come to fully manifest our potential for ourselves and for the world. This will be done if we have the strength to not only get through difficult times but to elevate through them.

How do we know when the tests will come? There were only ten instances in Abraham's long life that brought him to a new level of spiritual elevation. Imagine if Abraham had said at any one of those moments, "I won't take this opportunity, I'll wait for the next one." The truth is that we can never really be sure which one of those moments is the one that will take us to the next level of fulfilling our purpose in the world. The only thing we can do is make sure we pursue every opportunity so as not to miss a single one.

The Rav has made this very clear: We are not reading the Torah to remind ourselves of historical facts. *The Zohar* explains that the process Abraham and Isaac were going through in the Binding was a preparation for us and for the world. Through their consciousness, their work, and their ability to completely give up their *Desire to Receive for the Self Alone*, they made it possible for us to do our work.

Every time in our lives that we have the ability to hurt someone but we do not do so, every time we desire to be reactive but we resist that desire, we are partaking of the Light of the Binding of Isaac. That event created the ability for humanity to act with resistance, thus removing the *Desire to Receive for the Self Alone*.

It wasn't just that by "doing their share" that Abraham and Isaac resisted the *Desire to Receive for the Self Alone*. They did much more. They created a channel such that every action of resistance and every act of sharing in any time or place partakes of that Light. But if we do not think of drawing those two souls into our lives for the coming year, we will not be able to accomplish what we need to accomplish this year.

The Rav says people need bells and whistles, but the truth is always simple. The Binding of Isaac, which was the greatest act of resistance, opened the channel that allows all of us to resist. If we experience anger, selfishness, fear, or chaos in our lives, it's because we have not made a strong enough connection to these two great souls and to the channel they opened up for all of humanity. It really is just that simple. We need to say only one thing: "I know you are here, Abraham and Isaac, and you are opening the channel for restriction and removal of judgment. I want you to come into me." If we have that consciousness, they will come.

The Zohar also speaks about the ram that was sacrificed after the Binding of Isaac and about the reason we use the horn of a ram for the *shofar*. The sound of the horn does three things. First, it awakens that part of our soul that remains perfect, no matter what we have done or think we have done. The voice of the *shofar* not only awakens that spark of perfection but makes it flow through our soul and body so that it permeates our entire being.

Secondly, the *shofar* awakens the level of *Binah*, the Tree of Life. *Binah* then envelops us like the protective power of water envelops us in the *mikveh* (spiritual cleansing bath). The kabbalists teach that when we pray for another person and envelop them with our soul, our essence, and our being, they are literally not there anymore—they are covered by us. When we envelop them with our mind, heart, and soul, judgment cannot find them because they are not there anymore. They are enveloped by our Light. On Rosh Hashanah, we experience envelopment through the blowing of the *shofar*. We are enveloped by the Light of *Binah* and the Tree of Life.

The third level that we awaken through the blowing of the *shofar* is the ultimate level of redemption. Certainly, we think about ultimate redemption for ourselves and our loved ones, but we must also think about it for the whole world. The power awakened through the blowing of the *shofar*, which is the Light of *Binah*, will ultimately bring an end to pain and suffering everywhere.

The sound of the *shofar* is the human heart crying out. All the pain of humanity is awakened through that sound, taking us a step closer to the revelation of the great Light. This is why *The Zohar* says that the Negative Side becomes frightened by the sound of the *shofar*. It is afraid this may be the year the Final Redemption is revealed.

As we approach Rosh Hashanah, foremost in our minds must be our awareness of our true essence. We have infinite power within our souls. We need to keep this understanding—this awareness of how amazing every one of us is—throughout the year. We have to remind others and ourselves that our genuine essence is abundance and fulfillment, and our true work is to remove the barriers and veils we have put in their way. At Rosh Hashanah, we gain miraculous power to remove those veils.

There is an amazing sentence in one of Rav Brandwein's letters to the Rav. Rav Brandwein wrote: "Miracles don't happen." What can this possibly mean? Since so many of us are hoping for miracles, why did Rav Brandwein tell the Rav that miracles don't happen?

As Rav Brandwein went on to explain, if our consciousness is such that we believe things *can't* change, but then they *do* change, we believe it must have taken a miracle to make that change happen. When our consciousness is one of uncertainty, a miracle will always be surprising. As the kabbalists tell us, literally every breath we take is a miracle.

We can pray and hope for a miracle, but Rav Brandwein says that whatever happens within that frame of reference isn't really a miracle. If we had true consciousness of the potential for our soul to travel back to the Thought of Creation, we wouldn't think that anything is beyond the power of the Light to transform.

At Rosh Hashanah we need awareness of the fact that there are no miracles. If we truly know that life—our family, our business, every aspect of our life—is sustained by the Light of the Creator, we would never be surprised. Miracles are nothing but a different manifestation of the Light of the Creator, and realizing that fact is a matter of consciousness.

To help us understand this and to help us see clearly the nature of our work at Rosh Hashanah, I would like to share a story about two great kabbalists. As they were getting older they made a pact. If one passed away before the other, he would come back and tell what is happening in the next world.

Then one of them passed away, and his friend waited for a dream or a vision to reveal what awaits us in the other world. He waited for weeks and months, but nothing happened. Then by coincidence, he met the son of his friend who had died and he told the son about the pact and his disappointment.

That night, the son had a dream. In his dream, he went to the Heavens and said he wanted to see his father. He went into one chamber, and the souls in the chamber said, "Yes, we saw him, but he walked past." There were chambers beyond chambers, and the son kept walking and walking through one to the next until he came to the edge of a great, dark forest. He walked on, driven by the desire to see his father. He walked and he walked, and then finally he saw his father standing at the edge of an ocean, leaning on his cane and staring at the water. He went to his father and said, "What are you doing here? We were expecting you to tell us what is happening in the next world."

His father said, "Do you know what this ocean is? This is the ocean of all the tears that have been cried throughout history by all of humanity. I have told the Creator that I'm not leaving this ocean until He dries up all those tears."

At Rosh Hashanah we can connect with the power to dry those tears and to end all the pain and suffering of humanity once and for all. On Rosh Hashanah, through the gift Abraham and Isaac prepared for us, we can usher in the true and ultimate Redemption. We must have no doubt that in this year the Light is heralding not only our personal redemption but the very removal of death itself.

In this year the Creator will wipe away all our tears. This needs to be our consciousness. We have been given the power of the Binding of Isaac and the power of the *shofar* to awaken our inner soul. But our consciousness needs to be focused and true. We must use the gifts of Rosh Hashanah to bring about the Ultimate Redemption, the wiping away of all the tears.

CHAPTER 13

Yom Kippur

Yom Kippur is a tremendous opportunity to connect with the Light of *Binah* (our Supernal Mother) in a way that is not possible at any other time. The Rav has a perfect way of expressing this. The Rav always says, "On Yom Kippur, the energy store, the bank is open." Light that manifests in our lives as total fulfillment and as removal of any pain or lack is here for the taking on this day. There is no other day of the year when the gates of that wellspring are as open as they are on Yom Kippur.

The size of our Vessel on Yom Kippur determines how much Light will be able to enter. The way to enlarge our Vessel is to purify it, and on Yom Kippur, we are given the gift of being able to wash away our negativity. We immerse ourselves in the pool of the Light of *Binah*, the source of cleansing and blessings. Kabbalah tells us that for every Effect, there is a Cause. If any negativity manifests in our lives, it's because we have done something of a negative nature. Therefore, we must examine every one of our negative actions at Yom Kippur if we want to build a great Vessel and to make sure there are no holes. If there is a negative act that we have not acknowledged, that becomes a hole in our Vessel. As long as there is a hole, no matter how great the Light that will flow from our connection to *Binah*, we will not be able to sustain that Light.

The Zohar says that the only way to cleanse our negativity is to remember those aspects of ourselves that we want to send away, that we want to cleanse. It says that those negative actions that we remember will be forgotten on Yom Kippur and those that we forget will be remembered.

In order to partake of the blessings of *Binah*, we need to think about every aspect of our lives, about literally every action we have taken that has hurt another person, along with the aspect of ourselves that we want to cleanse. If we do not think about these, they will not be cleansed.

As we think about these actions, the power of the "*mikveh*" of *Binah*, of Yom Kippur, will cleanse those away. It is important that we remember them, awaken them, and let them be cleansed by the Light and the mercy of *Binah*. As Rav Ashlag explains in *Ten Luminous Emanations*, not only can we remove our negativity but we can also transform that negativity into Light.

Depending on how large our Vessel is and on the level of our consciousness, each of us will experience Yom Kippur differently. The more clarity we have, the more Light we will receive, and this in turn will result in the complete removal of any negativity we have already brought into our lives or that might otherwise be intended for us in the future.

In short, at Yom Kippur we need to maximize awareness of our connection to *Binah*. When we do this, *The Zohar* teaches that we will gain freedom from all chaos in our lives, both major and minor. We will also enjoy freedom from any type of suffering. All negative actions will be removed, along with all pain that we have brought others.

Like a *mikveh* (spiritual cleansing bath), Yom Kippur is an immersion that can completely remove every attachment of negativity. But the negativity can be released only if we are completely immersed. If even one hair stays out of the water, the negativity can remain attached. This is why we do not connect to the physical world on Yom Kippur. Our desire and consciousness, our constant meditation, is to be completely immersed in the Light of *Binah*.

At Yom Kippur there are five specific connections we need to make in order to advance to the next spiritual level. Although we abstain from eating food during Yom Kippur, these connections are five *spiritual* meals that elevate us. Like the rungs of a ladder, they allow us to move from our present level to a higher one.

The reason we don't eat on Yom Kippur is not because we want to punish ourselves. Rather, it's because on this day we don't want to connect in any way to the physical world. This is also why most of us don't wear leather shoes on Yom Kippur. It is a way to make sure we don't miss the amazing gift of this holiday. Our consciousness needs to be totally focused on the opportunity to connect to *Binah*.

To understand the Light that is available to us on Yom Kippur—not just to grasp it intellectually but to really awaken the Light in our heart and soul—we should read from *The Zohar*. The words of *The Zohar* are the means to awaken this Light. In reading and listening, we are awakening the Light of Yom Kippur for ourselves and for the world.

The Zohar says: "Come and see, on the day of Rosh Hashanah, *Malchut* is concealed. The Light of *Malchut* does not shine until the tenth day of the month. On the day of Yom Kippur, all people, or those who know, have cleansed themselves of the negativity, have done the process of *teshuvah*, of returning, and *Binah*, our Supernal Mother, shines down to *Malchut*, which is our Vessel. On Yom Kippur the Light of *Binah* shines so brightly that there is joy, not only in this world but in all the worlds. That is why Yom Kippur is referred to in plural terms, as *Yom HaKippurim*."

The Zohar goes on to ask: "Why do we give so much strength, so much importance, to the Negative Side on Yom Kippur?" On Yom Kippur, the Negative Angel (Satan) is calmly waiting for us to recount all those negative things we have done. We think about them, we say them, and we give them over to him. The negative angel thinks he will take all that negativity and bring it down onto us for this coming year. But fortunately for us, he doesn't understand the power of Yom Kippur.

Two things now occur. First, we awaken all that negativity, all those memories of what we have done wrong. The Hebrew words we speak are codes to awaken what we remember and even things we've forgotten. We give all of this negativity over to the Negative Side.

The second step is something that the Negative Side doesn't expect. We shield, bathe, and clothe ourselves in the overwhelming Light of *Binah* that is available on Yom Kippur. Because of this, the Negative Angel has no place to enter, no means of access. He can no longer bring that negativity back to us.

The first part of the Torah reading on Yom Kippur speaks about the death of Nadav and Avihu, the two children of Aaron. Why? We know there are no coincidences, so there must be a reason for this story preceding the discussion of the process of Yom Kippur. We also know that Yom Kippur is the death anniversary of Rav Akiva and the death anniversary of Rav Ashlag. That is no coincidence either. But how can we understand all this and put it together?

The kabbalists tell us that when Rav Akiva was taken captive by the Romans, they flayed the skin from his body with steel combs. They wanted to make his death as painful as possible.

As Rav Akiva was dying, he began to recite the *Kriat Shema*. He said, "All my life, I have been waiting and worrying about this verse, which speaks about giving ourselves over completely. When will I be able to completely do this process? Now I have the opportunity. How can I give it up?" As Rav Akiva ended the *Shema*, his soul departed. Kabbalists explain that every spiritual action is meant to completely unite us with the Light of the Creator. In the same way, the core of Rav Ashlag's teaching was the concept of *devechut*, which loosely translated means "complete union with the Light of the Creator."

True kabbalists completely give themselves over to the Creator in every connection they make. They create that union, that *devechut*, in every action. Their entire being, their entire soul, goes into that action. When they come to the morning connection, they put all of their life force into that connection. So how do they even stay alive after the prayer? How do their souls, which they have completely given over, reunite with their bodies? Every act of sharing has within it the power to achieve complete *devechut*, complete union with the Light of the Creator. The kabbalists teach that within this action is Light and that Light returns the soul to the body.

The only reason their souls come back to their bodies is because the Light of the Creator shines back into them. This is a struggle for truly righteous people, who must hold themselves back to keep their souls in their bodies. For a kabbalist, a truly righteous person, the physical body limits their ability to connect to the Light. They never want to return to their physical selves after they make a connection, but the Creator says, "You still have a job to do in your body."

When Rav Akiva was saying the *Kriat Shema*, he injected his entire being into this connection. He saw the Romans were in the process of physically killing his body so he seized the opportunity. He said, "Now there is no reason to limit myself anymore. The Romans are ending my physical being anyway." He told his students, "I'm not going to hold back anymore. Today I am going to make that connection complete." Rav Akiva's soul left his body as he uttered the word *echad* (one). Thus he achieved complete unity with God. The beauty of this is that he was not doing anything different than usual. His soul left his body every time he made a connection to the Light of the Creator because he always achieved complete union. But throughout Rav Akiva's life, the Creator kept pushing him back. The Creator said, "You still have work to do." But on the day of Yom Kippur, there was to be no pushing back. On this day, Rav Akiva created for us the power of complete and lasting *devechut*.

So on Yom Kippur we connect with *Binah*, to the Holy of Holies. This is a personal process that each of us needs to go through. What's more, we then continue the process as if we were with the High Priest walking into the Holy of Holies. As we enter with him, we are completely shielded by the Light of *Binah*, and negativity is forced to remain with the Negative Side. When we understand this process, we have grasped the gift of Yom Kippur. We have the power to awaken all the negativity that is part of us, to give it over, and to never have it come back to us. There is no other day of the year when we can so completely accomplish this task.

Nadav and Avihu, the sons of Aaron, also made the ultimate connection. Their desire, their feeling, their singular purpose for going into the Holy of Holies, was to unite completely with the Light of the Creator. On this day, they accomplished the work that every one of us has to do. They achieved the level of *devechut* with the Creator. But because it was not part of what was supposed to occur, there was no pushback: The Creator did not tell them they had work left to do in the world, their souls left their bodies.

Through the channel that Nadav and Avihu created, we can connect to the awesome power of Yom Kippur. If we want to have protection from all the negativity we have ever created, we have to connect to *Binah*, and we can connect to *Binah* through Nadav and Avihu.

I cannot tell you how excited I am about this understanding. This puts all the pieces into place. This is the one day of the year in which all people can achieve this level that Rav Ashlag wrote of and spoke about and begged that we make the object of our life's work. Yom Kippur is the day of complete *devechut*.

We awaken all our negativity, the barrier between ourselves and the Light, and give it all over to the Negative Side. And then we follow the channel Nadav and Avihu set up for us and bring the amazing Light of *Binah* that is Yom Kippur. Rav Akiva, Nadav and Avihu, and then Rav Ashlag all did the same thing on this day so that every single one of us can make this connection. To maximize the gift of this day, we need to make a deep connection with their souls. Then passing through the channels they created, we all enter into the Holy of Holies. We say *Ana Hashem* for the Creator, the letters of the word *Ana* (*Alef, Nun, Alef*) being an acronym for Eliyahu, Nadav, and Avihu.

To sum up, there are three very exciting gifts on this day: The opening of the bank of blessings; the cleansing of our negativity in the *mikveh* of *Binah*; and the transformation of all our negative actions into Light. As *The Zohar* says, without consciousness, without awareness, we will not be able to partake of these gifts.

CHAPTER 14

Sukkot

Sukkot brings a truly wonderful opportunity that is present at no other time of the year. A unique quality of spiritual Light is now available to us. In Hebrew, this Light is called *Or Makif,* which can be translated as "Encircling or Surrounding Light." Through both our actions and our consciousness at Sukkot, we can draw this powerful energy of protection and mercy for the entire year to come.

To bring this about, we should be aware of a key spiritual principle: *like attracts like.* A particular kind of energy manifesting in the material world draws a corresponding energy from the spiritual realm. More specifically, there are two channels of energy that we should utilize during the week of Sukkot, in our words and in our deeds, in order to create a connection to the extraordinary emanation of Light that is available.

First, we need to express kindness and sharing in everything we do. The *Or Makif*, the Surrounding Light, is the very essence of kindness and sharing. By bringing these qualities into our lives, both in our dealings with other individuals and in our dealings with the world as a whole, we will create a connection to the Surrounding Light that manifests mercy and sharing likewise for us. And again, we should be aware that these gates are open to that Light only at the time of Sukkot.

Secondly, this is a week in which there's great reason to be filled with joy. Here again the principle of "like attracts like" makes it very important that we experience this joy to the greatest extent possible. The Light of this week can't enter our lives without joy, just as it can't enter without sharing. Indeed, the kabbalists teach that the concepts of sharing and joy are intimately related. One leads to the other, and together they evoke the Light that awaits us during Sukkot.

With respect to both kindness and joy, however, it's not just our actions that draw forth the Light. The awareness that accompanies our acts is equally important. We need to be conscious of the feelings that motivate our deeds, and most importantly, we should be conscious of the Light that we are bringing to ourselves and to those we love.

The lessons and the Light for Sukkot do not come to us just so that we can be "good" or "spiritual" people. They are given to us in order to create very real, practical benefits of protection and mercy that can truly enrich our lives, the lives of our loved ones, and the lives of all humanity. The Surrounding Light is here for us at Sukkot, and we should make the most of this amazing opportunity.

CHAPTER 15

Rosh Chodesh Cheshvan

The month of Cheshvan, with its astrological sign of Scorpio, is often viewed as difficult. *The Zohar* describes Cheshvan as a time when challenges can arise. Following the month of Tishrei with all its holidays and cosmic openings, Cheshvan can seem a relatively dark time, a letdown from the previous month. Since there are no holidays in Cheshvan, it is often viewed as a negative period. But we know that sometimes the greatest potential exists when things appear darkest. That's certainly true in this month.

The Tetragrammaton combination for Cheshvan, the four channels through which the Light of the Creator flows down to us and to this world is: *Vav, Hei, Hei,* and *Yud.* The first point to notice about this combination is that the two instances of the letter *Hei,* the feminine side, which represent *Binah* and *Malchut,* are enclosed on one end by the *Vav* and on the other by the *Yud.* These are the two male aspects, signifying that the feminine aspect of the manifestation of the Light of the Creator is enveloped and protected by the male aspect.

As the kabbalists explain, in this month there is an element of challenge. Every one of us will probably feel it. But we also have the *Vav* and the *Yud* protecting our more vulnerable, feminine side. So when we look at Cheshvan's combination of letters—*Vav, Hei, Hei,* and *Yud*—we understand that meditating on these letters gives us the ability to protect and elevate ourselves from any challenge or difficulty we may experience during this month.

Certainly, whenever we encounter difficulties, it's important to remember one of the most important lessons that I've learned from the Rav, my father: that although there are going to be difficult situations in life, as long as we have certainty that eventually the outcome will be positive, we won't worry so much about how we are going to get there. This is a key understanding for us to keep in mind during Cheshvan. When we connect with and meditate on the tool of the *Vav, Hei, Hei,* and *Yud,* we will have certainty of the final positive outcome, despite any interim ups and downs.

When we are certain that the ultimate end of each process will be positive, the fact that there are challenges will not faze us. This is why the Tetragrammaton for this month ends with the *Yud,* which we know is the seed and the place from which all blessings, all great manifestations come from. So in constructing this code in this way, the kabbalists are teaching us that the end is in the beginning and that the positive beginning is also at work in the end, so there is nothing to worry about.

The numerical value of the letters *Chet, Shin, Vav, Nun* that spell the word *Cheshvan* (8+300+6+50=364) give us an understanding of the power of Cheshvan. As we know, there is one day of the year when Satan hangs out a sign on the door that states: "Left for vacation. Gone for the day." That day is Yom Kippur. Satan, with his chaos, can only reign 364 days of the year, not 365. The Rav reveals to us that this month of Cheshvan, because of its numerical value of 364, connects us to the essence of Yom Kippur and to the essence of what is called the Light of *Binah* that is available on Yom Kippur.

In *The Book of Formation*, Abraham explains which letter, and therefore what type of energy, brought each month into being and still continues to be available in that month. Abraham wrote that the Creator used the letter *Nun* to create the human sense of smell. The sages teach that Adam and Eve used only four of the five senses when the sin of Adam took place. They did not use their sense of smell. This means that the sense of smell is the most elevated and pure of the senses.

In many of our spiritual connections we use our sense of smell. For example, when the Shabbat comes to a close each Saturday night, we smell the myrtle branch or other Havdalah spices, which strengthens our soul. How does this relate to each of us? Although we may have done negative things, whether by hurting others or damaging ourselves and our connection to the Light of the Creator, there is always an element of our soul that remains untouched.

This is a very important understanding. Very often those of us who are involved in spiritual work look at ourselves and say,

"Well, I've done this and that wrong and acted this way and that way toward that other person." The list for every person can be endless, so do we really deserve the Light of the Creator?

This month shows us that the sense of smell has a spiritual significance: it reminds us that every single one of us has a spark within us that is never damaged, no matter what we have done. From that spark we know that we will always have the ability to connect to the Light of the Creator and to share it with others. The kabbalists point out that thoughts of our negativity and unworthiness are themselves from the Negative Side. We must neither forget nor doubt that part of our essence that *is never* damaged and *can never be* damaged. There is a part of our soul that always deserves and can always make a connection to the Light.

After creating the sense of smell, God created the sign of Scorpio, again through the letter *Nun*. What does this tell us? We know that the Hebrew word *nefilah* which means "falling," begins with the letter *Nun*. As mentioned previously in the chapter on Rosh Chodesh Nissan, this is the one letter of the Hebrew alphabet that is not present in the *Ashrei* prayer.

The gift of Cheshvan is the ability to fall and then to rise again. In this month we have the ability to descend through the process and elevate at the end because while the *Ashrei* contains every letter *except* the *Nun*, in the month of Cheshvan, the *Nun* is *not* missing. The reason is very clear: We cannot complete our work, we cannot elevate to the highest levels, without first going down and then going up. In this month, in order to achieve great blessings, we must connect to the letter *Nun*, and therefore, in this month, *Nun* is a channel for positive energy and for growth. So in Cheshvan when challenges come, we shouldn't run away from them because if we don't come across them and face them head on, we won't be able to ultimately grow. This month is not a time to shy away from difficulty; it is a month to grab the *Nun* and race towards the challenges, knowing that we can transform all of them and elevate even higher each time we fall.

When the Rav, my father, was living in the United States and Rav Brandwein, his teacher, was living in Israel, they would often speak on the phone and correspond through letters. In one such letter, Rav Brandwein taught the Rav and all of us a very important lesson: The Light cannot rest with darkness. Rav Brandwein wrote: "Blessings cannot come together with curses. In order to draw more Light—to draw more fulfillment and more blessings into our lives—we need to be of Light. We need to be like the Creator. We cannot draw the Light of the Creator into our lives unless we are like the Light of the Creator."

That's an interesting conundrum because it implies that if we are not yet completely connected to the Light of the Creator, we can't receive more Light. But if we can't receive more Light, how can we become more like the Creator? How can we draw more Light into our lives? If blessings cannot rest with curses and if Light cannot manifest with darkness, then how do we draw more blessings into our life when we are not yet perfect, when we are not yet connected to the Light?

In answer to these questions, Rav Brandwein explains that what we need to do is borrow from our own perfection. The kabbalists teach that each one of us is guaranteed to achieve perfection. Every single one of us will perfect our soul and will connect completely to the Light of the Creator. Every single one of us will eventually be fulfilled. We will receive the fulfillment and blessings for which we are brought into this world.

How long that process will take is something that only we can determine. It may take us a day, or a year, or fifty years, or even many lifetimes. But once we know that the end is guaranteed, that every single one of us will achieve that perfection, then, as Rav Brandwein explains, we can draw upon that connection. We can draw upon our own future perfection.

We know, as the kabbalists teach, that time—the concept of today, yesterday, and tomorrow—is an element that exists only in this physical world. The spiritual world, the Supernal World, does not operate within the framework of time's limitations. There is no time, space, or motion in the spiritual world. That means that the ultimate perfection that will be achieved by us at some point in time can actually be connected to right now.

This is one of the key teachings of Rav Ashlag in *The Ten Luminous Emanations*. There is no time, space, and motion at the highest level of reality. So the perfection that each one of us is guaranteed to achieve some time in the future is actually, in the spiritual world, already a fact. We can connect to that perfection at this very moment. We can draw upon that perfection to help us in the physical world. What an exciting, amazing concept this is! At this exact moment, every single one of us can connect to our perfected self, to the self that is completely connected to the Light, completely at peace, and completely fulfilled.

Not only can we do this, as Rav Brandwein explains, but we *need* to do this. If we want to draw more Light into our life, connecting to our perfected self is the first step. We must know in our consciousness that we *can* do this and that we *will* do this. Then we can draw that perfection and use what Rav Brandwein calls our "borrowed Vessels" to draw Light.

This means that anytime I am in a situation where I want more Light—whether it is in my relationship with my children, with my wife, with my family; whether it's in business or in any aspect of my life where I want more blessings—I can have those blessings immediately because I actually already have them in the Supernal Realm.

Of course, there needs to be a meditation to connect to our perfected self that precedes the drawing of the Light. If we want to draw Light, if we want to draw blessings, we must have a Vessel that the Light can enter into. That Vessel is our perfected self. This is a very basic understanding. Without it, Rav Brandwein explains we can't draw the maximum volume of Light. We can draw a limited amount of Light, but if we want to draw boundless Light and endless blessings, then we need to connect to our perfected self.

Once again, the Negative Side will demand of us whether we really deserve to achieve perfection. Do we really believe that we deserve to have complete fulfillment? But we do deserve it because in the spiritual world, in the metaphysical world beyond our five senses, there is the perfection that we have already achieved. Our perfected self is already there. Every single one of us is perfect at this very moment. Through our meditation and our consciousness, we simply need to connect to that perfected self. Then, through those borrowed Vessels, we can draw all the boundless Light into our life. But until we begin to connect to our perfected self, until we begin to understand the concept of "borrowed Vessels" and connect to that reality, we can only draw a limited amount of Light.

This month of Cheshvan, this month of Scorpio, this month of *Nun* and of *nefilah*, has within it the gift for every single one of us to connect to our perfected self. Simply grasping this fact brings immense encouragement for reaching our ultimate goal. Once we understand the power of this month, we not only acquire the Vessel but also the ability to draw endless blessings and Light into the Vessel of our life. So during Cheshvan, whether it's every day or every two days or however often we choose, we need to take the time to meditate, to think, to strengthen our consciousness of our perfected self. As Rav Brandwein writes, it is through our awareness and our consciousness and our meditation that we create a borrowed Vessel through which endless Light can enter our lives. But unless we utilize this gift of the borrowed Vessels, the amount of Light that we draw into our lives will be limited.

I hope we're now beginning to see that the entire month of Cheshvan is a tremendous opportunity to connect with the *Sfirah* of *Binah*, the energy shield that can protect us from all darkness and negativity. The Rav has often discussed this point. To understand this concept, the Rav has made it very clear that consciousness is the key to connection.

Unfortunately, we may find ourselves thinking, "If connection is only about consciousness, it seems too easy." But the Rav stresses time and again that consciousness is the key. For the majority of us, it may seem impossible that with just a simple thought, we can remove chaos from our life—but that's what the Negative Side wants us to think. As long as we remain convinced that chaos is permanently built into our life's processes, then there is no way that we can ever eliminate chaos. But we are coming into a new age of awareness when we, with our consciousness, can determine that the Negative Side will no longer have any control over us.

The Rav speaks about the fact that the kabbalists refer to the month of Scorpio as *Mar Cheshvan*. The word *mar* means "bitter," and many commentaries explain that Cheshvan is called bitter because the Great Flood discussed in the Book of Genesis occurred during this month. But the Rav, as always, does not take any explanation at face value and asks why Abraham, in *The Book of Formation,* specifically chose the moment of the Flood to be in the month of Scorpio, since many historic catastrophes occurred at various other times of the year. The Rav also asks, "Why was this month chosen specifically to be called bitter?"

Then the Rav looks even deeper. The Rav tells us that on this night of Rosh Chodesh Cheshvan we have the opportunity to take care of all the other days of the year. But once again, maybe it seems too simple. Can it really be that in this month our consciousness can transform *mar* (bitter) into its reverse, *ram*, which in English means "exalted" and "powerful?" Yes, it really is just that simple, and the Rav stresses that fact again and again. Why do we always question the simple truths of life? Our questioning is the Negative Side's most formidable weapon. "It's too good to be true" is negativity's most powerful pronouncement!

We now come to what I think is the Rav's most exciting revelation for this month of Cheshvan. When many of us read the story of the Flood in the Bible, we imagine a terrible calamity with water spread all over the world, eliminating all life. But the kabbalists never accept the literal explanation of biblical teachings. The Rav says that the story about the Flood in the Bible is not about a terrible watery darkness that comes down to our world. Quite the opposite. Through the channel of *Chesed,* of mercy, our world drew what was necessary for it at that time—and is still very necessary. It drew a flood of kindness, a flood of mercy. That was the true essence of the energy revealed during the Flood, and that is the energy that is revealed in Cheshvan every year.

This is an amazing and beautiful understanding. The month of Cheshvan is not a time when water was used to destroy. It is a time when a flood of mercy came down to our world, and that is the tremendous opportunity that we can take advantage of in this month. To remove the permanent chaos from our lives, God called upon the cleansing power of water. Water was chosen to heal the world, not to destroy it. The Deluge came about to rid the world of all the chaos that existed at that time. There was no other choice then, just as there is no other choice today. We must be cleansed because we have no other alternative if we hope to bring fulfillment into our lives.

We have learned several secrets here, but if we remember only one thing, it is to replace "I *want* to share" with "I *need* to share because it is in my interest to do so, so that I can achieve my potential." In this month, as in no other month of the year, there is the potential for *ram*, for greatness, but only if we live every day of this month with the understanding that the Rav has given to us. We have no other choice but to be a person of sharing. We have no other choice but to show mercy and kindness. It is not because we want to be good people, not because we want to be spiritual people. If we want to receive all the Light that is available in this month, if we want to receive all the blessings that are available for ourselves and for our families and for those around us in all areas of our lives, we have no other choice but to be sharing people. And if we do that, if we understand the opportunity of this month, then truly every single one of us will have not a *Mar Cheshvan*, but an exalted and powerful *Ram Cheshvan*.

CHAPTER 16

Rosh Chodesh Kislev

The kabbalists refer to the month of Kislev (Sagittarius) as the month of miracles. This certainly is going to be a departure from the previous month, the month of Cheshvan (Scorpio), in which we often find ourselves dealing with challenges and facing up to difficult situations.

During this month we can draw the energy we will need for the rest of the year in order to create miracles in our lives. But before we can begin using the energy of Kislev, there is a certain level of consciousness we must have. This is what we should focus on for this month.

Whenever we try to understand a particular month, it is helpful to turn to the *Sefer Yetzirah, The Book of Formation*. There, Abraham the Patriarch revealed many secrets, including the means by which letters of the ancient Hebrew alphabet are used to connect with certain energies. Abraham tells us that the Creator took the letter *Samech*, and through the energy and power of that letter created the sign of Sagittarius in the month of Kislev.

We also know that the kabbalists assign a specific combination of the Tetragrammaton letters of *Yud, Hei, Vav*, and *Hei* to every month, allowing us to draw specific aspects of the Light for that month. For Kislev, the combination is *Vav, Yud, Hei*, and *Hei*.

So we will use these two tools—the letter *Samech*, with which this month was created, and the Tetragrammaton combination of *Vav, Yud, Hei*, and *Hei*—to meditate upon and to draw the Light for Kislev, a month of miracles for ourselves and for the world.

As the Rav has explained, the special energy of this month was available before Chanukah, before the great miracle of the small army defeating a large one. The Creator formed this month with the tools, with the energy, with the ability to create miracles. No physical reality can ever affect the prior consciousness that brought about the physical reality in the first place. Therefore, Chanukah, the miracle of Lights and all that this entails, was the Effect rather than the Cause of Kislev being called the month of miracles.

And concerning this, the kabbalists ask two important questions: "What is the reason for the Light of Chanukah continuing throughout history? What is the singular reason that this Light continues to permeate our world?"

To answer these questions, let's look more closely at exactly what took place at Chanukah. First, the tiny insignificant army of Israelites defeated a great army of the enemy and drove that army out of the land. The Israelites then entered the Temple that had been ransacked. The menorah in the Temple, which was always supposed to be kept alight, was not lit, and much of the Temple had been damaged. The Israelites didn't know if they could find oil for the menorah because this was very special oil created in a unique way. But as they were walking through the Temple, they found a small jar of oil.

We all know the rest of the story. There was only enough to oil to light the *menorah* for one day, but the menorah remained lit for eight days. That miracle—that one small jar of oil kept the *menorah* alight for eight days—is the basis for Chanukah, and it is the energy of this miracle that we connect to every year at this time. But if we look at this logically, it doesn't make any sense. What is the real miracle: the oil or the battle?

Imagine if you were to tell someone: "You have two miracles in front of you. You have to decide which is greater and which is smaller. In one, thousands of people were about to be killed by a great army that was coming. But a very small number of people were able to defeat that army and survive. That's the first miracle. The second miracle is the finding of a small jar of oil that was able to keep the *menorah* of the Temple lit for eight days."

Clearly, the more significant miracle was the small army defeating the greater army and the thousands of people escaping death. Why, then, do the kabbalists say that the finding of the small jar of oil that should have been enough for only one day but lasted for eight is the more important? Why is this the pathway by which we connect to the Light of miracles in this month?

There is a very famous story in the Torah (Genesis 18:1-13) about Abraham and Sarah, who were very old and had no children. Throughout their entire lives, they had hoped for a child. One day, three travelers appeared at Abraham's tent in the desert. Of course, he invited them in and shared with them his hospitality. Then the travelers told Abraham, "Next year at this time, you will have a child."

The Torah says that when Sarah overheard this, she started laughing. This is perfectly understandable. She was in her nineties, and Abraham was a hundred years old. They had probably given up hope of having a child.

But then a very interesting thing happened. The Torah states the Creator became very upset at Sarah and asked her, "Why did you laugh?" Then the Creator went on to explain, "Is there anything that God cannot do?"

When the kabbalists look at this story, even in a very literal sense, they ask what seems to be an obvious question: Why the three strangers? If God had come to Sarah or to Abraham and promised them that next year at this time they would have a child, of course Abraham and Sarah would have had no doubt. Sarah's response would have been, "Of course I believe that there is nothing that God cannot do." But it wasn't God promising; it was just three strangers.

What is the Torah teaching us here? What lesson can we learn? The answer goes back to the original statement we looked at in the chapter on Rosh Hashanah: Miracles do not happen. To understand this, our view of the world needs to change. We need to change our perspective so we can bring what we call miracles into our lives.

If we look closely at this world—the sun rising in the morning and setting at night, and the moon coming out—we see that all of this is actually a manifestation of the Light of the Creator. The sun rises in the morning and sets at night, not because that is its "nature" but because the Light of the Creator gives it energy in the morning to shine and at night to be hidden. When we view nature as a manifestation of the Light of the Creator, we can understand that miracles are not really a departure from nature. Every birth is a miracle, whether the mother is twenty years old or ninety.

This is a basic understanding, especially as we try to draw miracles into our life, and Kislev is one of the most important months in which to have this consciousness. We need to change the way we view everything in this world, realizing that there is no fundamental distinction between "nature" and "miracles." There is only the infusion and the reinfusion of the Light of the Creator in our lives, which manifests in different ways. When we ask for miracles, all we're asking for is a different manifestation of the Light.

Specifically, we see here that miracles do not rest in an empty place. This is why consciousness and certainty are so crucially important. If there is no certainty, there is no opening: The Light doesn't have a place to enter. That's why we can never give up hope.

If Sarah had had this consciousness, she wouldn't have laughed when the three travelers told her that she would have a child the next year. In a sense, God was telling Sarah that she would never be able to have a child until her consciousness changed, and this is the lesson for us also. We need awareness that all of nature and all miracles are simply different manifestations of the Light of the Creator. But as long as we consider them two separate functions, we won't be able to draw the Light of miracles into our lives.

When the Rav was living in the United States and Rav Brandwein, his teacher, was living in Israel, they would stay in touch. The Rav would fly to Israel to be with Rav Brandwein, and they would speak on the phone. They also wrote letters, and in one of these letters, Rav Brandwein explains that miracles are based on a teaching of the Baal Shem Tov where he says that the Creator behaves towards us as we ourselves behave.

Literally, the Light of the Creator reflects our actions. In order for us to draw miracles into our life, we have to go against our selfish nature. To the degree that we go against our *Desire to Receive for the Self Alone*, we can change the nature of the world. The more we act against our *Desire to Receive for the Self Alone*, the more we can change the nature of the world.

The splitting of the Red Sea, for example, is one of the greatest miracles in the Bible. Rav Brandwein said that in order for this miracle to become manifest, the Israelites had to hugely go against their *Desire to Receive for the Self Alone*, against their ego. It was only when they were completely willing to give up their selfishness that they were they able to draw the great miracle, that of the splitting of the Red Sea.

The degree to which we act against our nature is the degree to which we can draw miracles into our lives. So if you need a miracle, make sure you act against your reactive nature. If you were going to get angry at your co-worker, at your family member, at your spouse, don't do it! By going against that reactivity, you create an opening for a miracle to come into your life. The greater your restriction, the more you resist the *Desire to Receive for the Self Alone*, the greater the opening for miracles in your life.

But perhaps the most important awareness that we need in order to draw miracles is the concept of appreciation. Everything in our lives is a manifestation of the Light of the Creator, but we have a huge tendency to take things for granted. We lose appreciation for what the Light has brought us and we focus instead on what we don't already have.

The Zohar says if people run after what is not theirs, they can lose what actually belongs to them. This is the lesson of appreciation. When we wake up in the morning and don't have tremendous joy because of all the blessings that we already have in our life and instead take these blessings for granted and assume that they are ours to keep, we are opening the door for that Light to be removed and for those blessings to be lost. And of course, we are also closing the door for any new Light and for any new miracles.

In this month of miracles, the first step must be to truly develop our appreciation for the Light and for those blessings that we already have. It is not simply because it is the right thing to do or it is the spiritual thing to do. It is because this consciousness, this awareness, this appreciation lets us hold onto those blessings of the Light that are manifest within what we have. If we truly have appreciation in our life, if we truly appreciate the way the Light of the Creator manifests in our life, we can never be sad. We can never be anything but filled with joy.

But it's not easy and it doesn't happen by itself. So often, for instance, when I'm putting my children to sleep and I'm lying there next to them, I suddenly realize the gift that I have. But what happens the next day? I may forget what I felt the night before, which is really unfortunate. Every single one of us has the ability to appreciate, and appreciation not only draws and sustains the Light but also opens the gate for more blessings.

So we now can begin to understand the energy that is available to us in this month. As we draw miracles into our life during Kislev, we need to remember three lessons. First, miracles do not just happen; what we call miracles is simply the presence of the Light of the Creator. Secondly, the way to draw miracles is by going against our ego-driven nature. And the third precept is appreciation: not only *having* appreciation, but *growing* appreciation. As we do this, we hold on to the blessings that we already have, and we also gain the power to draw new blessings and new miracles into our lives for ourselves and for the world.

CHAPTER 17

Chanukah

A unique kind of Light and a tremendous amount of blessings are ready to come into our lives specifically at Chanukah. Although Chanukah commemorates a historical event that took place thousands of years ago, it is much more than that.

We know that Chanukah is about miracles. We know that miracles occurred at this time of year at a certain point in history. Kabbalistically, we also know that Chanukah is a cosmic opening and opportunity for bringing miracles into our lives right now and for drawing the power of miracles for the rest of the year. To make this happen, we must be aware that any miracle, including the miracle of Chanukah, is an event that goes "beyond nature"—meaning beyond *our* nature. The only way that we can draw miracles is by going beyond and against our ego-driven nature. As long as we act within the confines of our ego, of our selfishness, of our *Desire to Receive for the Self Alone*, there will be a barrier between ourselves and the power of miracles.

As the kabbalists teach, the only way we can draw Light is by creating the correct Vessel. Without the Vessel, Light cannot become manifest, even though the Creator desires to share it with us. And without knowing the type of Light that is available, how can we create the proper Vessel? Therefore, at Chanukah, we must understand the codes that reveal the nature of this holiday's Light.

Each night of Chanukah, for example, we light one more candle than the night before until on the last night, we light all eight candles. If we add the number of candles—one on the first night, plus two on the second night, plus three on the third night, and so on—the number we reach is thirty-six, which is conveyed by the letters *Lamed*, *Vav*. These two letters spell the word *lev*, which means "heart." The kabbalists explain that this is not coincidental. It tells us what kind of Light is being revealed at this time. Once we know this, we can prepare a Vessel to receive this Light.

The truth is that the Vessel is always the missing piece of the puzzle. The Light is always ready to give, but often the Vessel is not there to receive the Light. When we discuss Chanukah, it is important to first grasp the fact that the Light is definitely available. The next step is, understanding exactly what type of Light, energy, and blessings are opened to us during these eight days.

The Light of the Creator functions as a mirror to us. As we act, we are acted upon. It's Cause and Effect. If we want something in our life to go beyond the laws of nature, beyond what will "naturally" occur in our lives, then we need to go beyond the confines our own nature, which in the physical world is our ego and the *Desire to Receive for the Self Alone*.

This is really a very simple and clear concept. At Chanukah, the Gates of Heaven are opened for miracles to come to us. But if we stay within our nature of *Desire to Receive for the Self Alone*, we restrict the type of miracle that can come into our lives. So during these eight days, we need to disconnect from our nature of selfishness. To the degree that we do that, miracles will happen for us.

A very beautiful section of *The Zohar* refers to what is called the *Or Haganuz*, or "the Concealed Light." Before the universe came into being, at the moment of the Thought of Creation, the Creator could see all of history in its totality, from the beginning of the universe until the Final Redemption and completion of humanity. The Creator saw that in order for the Final Redemption to occur, the pain and suffering that exists in our world had to be part of the process. There is a continuum of creation, leading up to the *Gamar Hatikkun* (the Final Correction), when pain, suffering, and death are finally removed from this world through the actions and consciousness of humanity as a whole. When the Creator created the world, He also foresaw the process through which mankind would have to be responsible for the perfection that this world is meant to achieve.

Therefore, the Creator realized that if the Light were completely revealed, without any barriers or veils in our world, we would have no free will or free choice because when we are completely connected to the Light, we can do nothing but good. We can do nothing of a negative nature. So there had to be a restriction and concealment of the Creator's Light from our world. But that Light didn't disappear. It was simply concealed, which is why it's called "the Concealed Light," the *Or Haganuz*.

In essence, the Concealed Light is everything that we as individuals are lacking and that is also lacking in the world as a whole. Every instance of pain in our lives and in the world exists only because the Concealed Light is not completely revealed. Our task, through our personal spiritual work and also through our global work, is to reveal more and more of that Concealed Light. When enough of that Light is revealed, the Final Correction will occur and pain and suffering will be completely removed from the world.

Once we understand this, we can see that every act of sharing, and every act of restricting our selfish reactive behavior, reveals more and more of the Concealed Light. This is what we need to strive for every day until a critical mass of Concealed Light is revealed and the Final Correction takes place. At Chanukah, the Concealed Light is revealed and opened for all of us in a way that does not occur at any other time. The Light is available not because we earned it, but because during these eight days, the Gates of Heaven are opened. Every pain that we feel, every illness, every difficulty and problem can now be washed away by the Light.

Once we understand this, we can take advantage of the beautiful and powerful opportunity of these eight days. Chanukah is our opportunity to bring the Light to those places of need. To the degree that we desire the Light, the Light will be revealed.

That's why the kabbalists explain that there is almost nothing required of us on Chanukah. On other holidays there are many prayers, meditations, and physical actions designed for drawing the Light. At Chanukah we light candles and that's all. There are certain additional prayers, but they're minimal. This is because the Light at Chanukah is so high and so powerful that there is almost nothing that we need to do in order to draw that Light. It is simply a gift. All that's required is the Vessel to receive it.

There is a story about one of the great kabbalists who asked people who came to him with their problems if they would write down their names and the difficulties they were facing on a piece of paper. The kabbalist would then meditate on what had been written.

One day, a man came to the kabbalist with two pieces of paper: one was his own piece of paper and the other was a paper from one of his friends. First he gave the kabbalist his own paper, and the kabbalist looked at it and meditated on his name. Then the man handed over his friend's paper. The kabbalists looked at it and said, "I see that this man's soul is shining with tremendous Light." Then he meditated on the friend's name and prayed for him.

A few months later, the same man came back to the kabbalist. Again, he presented the kabbalist with both his own name and that of his friend for the kabbalist to pray and meditate on. But this time when the kabbalist looked at the friend's name, he literally threw it out of his hands, shouting, "How could you bring me this man's name? He's such a negative person. I don't even want his name in my house!"

The visitor replied, "I'm very confused. A few months ago, I gave you that same person's name and you told me that his soul was shining with tremendous Light. Now you tell me that he's a terribly negative person."

The kabbalist thought for a few moments, then said, "I understand what happened. A few months ago when you first came in with that person's name, he was lighting the candles for Chanukah. And when a person lights the candles on Chanukah, no matter how negative he is and no matter how many negative actions he's done, the Light of Chanukah shines in his soul. Unfortunately, your friend didn't continue that connection with the Light when Chanukah was over. He gave it up. So now I see the true darkness that is in his soul."

The lesson for us here is to understand the immense power of Chanukah and the Concealed Light that it reveals. The more we appreciate how powerful this Light is and what it can do, the more Light we can bring into our lives. Once we believe our power to be a channel for the Light of the Creator, there is nothing that is beyond us. Now we can draw on the energy of Chanukah to remove the negative, insidious voice that tells us we are helpless, that we can't do great things. As the kabbalists explain, every single one of us is destined to become a limitless conduit for the Light of the Creator. Lighting the Chanukah candles shows us what our purpose in the world really is. It is to have the Light of the Creator in our lives. It is to illuminate candle after candle, and ultimately to bring the removal of all darkness forever.

CHAPTER 18

Rosh Chodesh Tevet

The month of Tevet, with its sign of Capricorn, is unique in that the month begins on the seventh day of Chanukah. The preceding month of Kislev is a time when we have the ability to draw miracles into our lives. That ability derives from the cosmic event of Chanukah, the channel for miracles, which now continues into Tevet.

Why does this happen? To understand the gifts and the challenges that are available for us in this month, the Rav explains from *The Zohar* that there are three months in which a great deal of judgment and negativity prevails. These are the months of Tammuz, Av, and Tevet. But it is not correct to see Tevet simply as a month of judgment. Indeed, there is a deeper, more powerful, and more important understanding given in the section of *The Zohar* concerning this month. Rather than being a negative month, Tevet is a month with an overabundance of Light.

Rav Ashlag has also discussed this principle. As he has written, during this time the *Shechinah*, the female aspect of the Creator present in our world, is not revealed. The *Shechinah* is not something that we can detect with our five senses, but *The Zohar* refers to the *Shechinah* as our "protective shield." Simply put, when the Shechinah is in place, it prevents us from receiving an overdose from the Lightforce of the Creator. Just as Earth needs the ozone layer to protect it from the sun, we also need protection from the infinite power of unfiltered Light. So rather than an absence of Light in this month, there an absence of the protective shield that usually limits the amount of Light that comes into our world.

With this understanding, we begin to have an inkling of what this month is about. It is a month with no filter and an overabundance of the revelation of the Light of the Creator. As we will see, this is a very positive opportunity, but it is also a time to be careful. The full impact of the Lightforce of the Creator creates too much Light, too much heat, which can result in all forms of destruction. The Rav has often made the point that, throughout history, Tevet has influenced people in negative ways. This is because people have succumbed to intolerance and *hatred for no reason* during this month. For those who practice intolerance, for those who do not share, for those who are selfish, this is a month when there is nothing to stop them. There is no filter preventing people who are disconnected from the Light from bringing judgment into their own lives.

All in all, this is a very serious month in which there is great opportunity but, at the same time, great danger. When a tremendous infusion of Light comes into an unprepared Vessel—into a person who is not ready for it, or who is acting with a lack of human dignity or with a lack of love towards another person—that Light causes a short circuit. That Light causes negativity.

So how can we make sure that our experience of this overflow of Light is positive? How can we be certain it will bring blessings into our lives?

The answer lies in our own consciousness and our own behavior. In this month, we must match the overabundance of Light with an overabundance of human dignity bestowed on others. We must foster an overabundance of sharing. We must have overwhelming love toward other people. In this way, we can connect to Tevet in a positive way and make positive use of Tevet's overabundance of Light.

During this month, the Creator chose the letter *Ayin* as the governing force of the sign Capricorn. *Ayin* is a letter that manifests the energy of anger. With the combination of the letter *Ayin* and the letter Bet, the sign of Capricorn and the month of Tevet were brought into being.

Of course, anger is something we all need to deal with every day, but it is an issue of particular concern during this month. (When we talk about the energy of a month, this pertains to everyone, not just to those who are born in that month.)

As we'll see, anger has both positive and negative sides, but the kabbalists tell us that no other emotion has the power to eliminate the Light the way anger does. I think most of us realize that anger can be a source of great negativity, and throughout this month, we need to see and understand the true danger of becoming angry.

The Zohar tells us there is almost nothing worse than a person reacting in anger. And the way to know whether to get close to someone or to stay away from them is to see how they become angry. Through witnessing a person's anger, we can literally determine the level of connection that the individual has with the Light of the Creator. And by considering your own anger, you can also determine the strength of your own connection. *The Zohar* says that when a person becomes angry, he literally throws away his soul, throws away his Light, and opens himself to darkness from the Other Side to come in its place.

Think of the times when something angers you. Think about the situations that make you angry or that make another person angry. If someone loses control during moments of anger, that person is not connected to the Light. As *The Zohar* explains, the action and reaction of anger literally disconnects us from the Creator's Light.

This is a very frightening concept. It should cause us to look seriously at the danger of bringing angry people into our lives, and even more importantly, to see the danger of being angry ourselves. That doesn't mean that we can instantly remove the possibility of ever becoming angry, but we can and should understand the danger of losing control through anger. *The Zohar* goes on to explain that the difference between anger and any other negative action is that when a person becomes angry, he literally internalizes darkness. That is why *The Zohar* says there is almost nothing a person can do of a negative nature that is as damaging as a person who loses his temper in anger.

The Zohar advises not to speak to such a person at this time. When we speak to someone who has lost his temper, it's as if we are directly connecting with the Negative Side because the anger has literally removed the Light from within the person. That disconnection from the Light is caused by the "fire of anger," which is just too dangerous to ignite. Of course, this is not a physical fire but rather an ignition from inside that literally burns away our connection to the Light of the Creator.

The next time we are about to become angry, the next time we're about to lash out at someone in anger, we should remind ourselves of the danger of what we're about to do. We are about to awaken a fire that will burn away a tremendous amount of Light, a tremendous amount of blessings, which we have worked hard for in growing our connection to the Light of the Creator.

It's important to understand the difference between reprimanding someone who's done something wrong and incorporating anger into the equation. We can never become angry, yet we all feel it. Some of us know when we've "lost it." We know when we've become angry; it happens many times each day. The second we feel it, when we feel that fire beginning to burn, we need to extinguish it right away. The damage that fire can do, the disconnection that fire can cause, is far too dangerous.

Anger is closely related to what Rav Ashlag, in his book *Gift of the Bible*, says about the ego, which he also calls the *Desire to Receive for the Self Alone*, or the Negative Side. At anger's core is an insidious energy, an essence that has become implanted within us that tells us, "You want this and you want that and you want to react in such and such a way." In so doing, it disconnects us from the Light of the Creator.

One of the biggest problems that we have in fighting our Negative Side is realizing that it's not really our Negative Side. The ego, the *Desire to Receive for the Self Alone, isn't really us.* Every reactive thought or feeling is a separate entity from our true being. We may think that it's *our* desire and *our* thought, but it isn't.

The voice of the Negative Side makes us think that we want to become angry, that we want to hurt that other person, that we want to be dominated by the power of ego. This is how the Negative Side gets us to disconnect from the Light.

But this, of course, is not what we really want at all. This voice that has taken root within us can be so convincing that we totally identify with it, especially in moments of anger. But Rav Ashlag writes that the whole purpose of our spiritual work is to realize that the ego, the *Desire to Receive for the Self Alone,* is not really us and is, in fact, our worst enemy. And anger is our worst enemy's most powerful weapon against us. Our Opponent makes us think this is what we want. He makes us perform his actions, creating negativity in our lives that will, whether two days later or two years later, come back and manifest as darkness.

I hope by now that the negative effects of anger are very clear. But what is the positive side of anger? As Rav Ashlag writes, there's only one thing that we must become more and more angry with, and that is the ego, the *Desire to Receive for the Self Alone,* the selfish thoughts and ideas that are always trying to invade our minds.

The first step is to realize that the ego is not us. You, and I, and every single one of us is pure Light. Our soul, our essence, is a complete connection to the Light of the Creator—the connection to the Light that brings all the blessings and all the fulfillment for which we came to this world. Once we see who we are and what the Other Side is, we have to begin separating ourselves from those negative thoughts. It's that simple.

The second step is to separate ourselves from the Negative Side, and that's a life's work. It's not something we can do in one day or even in a matter of years, but positive anger is a powerful tool we can use to speed up the process.

So in this month, we want to resist the tendency to become angry with other people, even if the ego tries to justify this anger in our minds. Instead, we want to awaken the great gift of this month, which is positive anger towards our ego and towards the *Desire to Receive for the Self Alone*.

When we consistently disassociate ourselves from our ego and become angry at it, we're truly on the path for which we came into this world, truly on the path toward the complete Light and blessings for which we came to this world.

Imagine if you knew, if you understood, if you remembered that the negative voice within you only wants to cause you harm. Think how different your life would be if you constantly recognized that enemy.

The gift of this month is the awareness of the test that we must pass—as well as the power to pass it. It's a month to completely remove anger and judgment, to awaken the positive and much more important anger that we need to fulfill our destiny. It's a month to become angry at the ego, to become angry at the *Desire to Receive for the Self Alone*. It's a month in which we can use the Opponent's own best weapons against him.

CHAPTER 19

Rosh Chodesh Shevat

For this month of Shevat, with its astrological sign of Aquarius, the Tetragrammaton combination is *Hei, Yud, Vav,* and *Hei.* Notice that this combination has the two letters *Hei* on the outside. The kabbalists teach that the letters *Yud* and *Vav* in the Tetragrammaton are the male aspects, while the two *Hei's* are female. *Hei* represents drawing down and manifestation of the Light of the Creator to this world. The male aspect represents potential rather than manifestation.

So this month has great potential for manifestation, which is expressed not only though the letters of the Tetragrammation but also through the letters that comprise the name of the month itself. Specifically, this involves the letter *Tzadi*. Abraham wrote in *The Book of Formation*: "With the energy and the Light of the letter *Tzadi*, the Creator made the month of Aquarius, which is called Shevat." Therefore, the letter *Tzadi* is the key to the abundance of Light that is available to be drawn to our world during Shevat.

We know that the Hebrew language was never meant to be the language of a specific people. Rather, it is an ancient universal tool through which we can unlock great energy. *The Zohar* tells us that before the creation of the world, each letter of the Hebrew alphabet came before the Creator and said, "Make the world through me." Each of the letters was saying, "Use my unique energy to create physical reality." And the letter *Tzadi* said to the Creator, "Create the world through me because the word for 'righteous' (*tzaddik*) begins with the letter *Tzadi*. Even You, God, have a name that begins with me." Then the Creator replied, "Yes, the word 'righteous' begins with the letter *Tzadi*, but your energy needs to be concealed because now is not the time for your revelation."

Indeed, the revelation of the letter *Tzadi* requires some close attention. The letter is made up of two different letters of the Hebrew alphabet. When we focus on the right side of the letter, we see the letter *Yud*, and of all the Hebrew letters, it is *Yud* that manifests connection to the ultimate Light of the Creator. The second half of the letter on the left-hand side is the letter *Nun*, which represents falling in every aspect. We fall out of favor. We fall into ill health. We fall from wealth into poverty. Falling includes everything that involves descending into a dimension that does not embrace happiness.

Rav Ashlag says that in the letter *Tzadi*, it's as if the *Yud* is turning away from the *Nun*. They are literally back to back, not face to face. Here, as always, the letter's appearance is very significant because this represents the spiritual energy that is flowing through the letter. The *Tzadi* represents our world as it is today, where there is, pain, suffering, and lack of harmony. When pain and suffering are finally removed from our world, the letters *Yud* and *Nun* will turn back toward each other and unite in love. But as long as there is darkness in our world, those two letters must be back to back because Light in its completion cannot yet be revealed.

When we focus on the *Nun*, that is, the lower half of the letter *Tzadi*, we inject into it all the times we have experienced spiritual falling as well as all the lack that we have in our lives. Today it might be a lack of health. Tomorrow it might be a lack in business, or in relationships, or in family. We take all that energy and we inject it into the letter *Nun*. Then we literally see the letter *Yud* enter and connect to the letter *Nun*. We see the *Yud* elevate all that falling and all that lack into a connection to the Light of the Creator. The beauty, then, of the combination of these two letters, the *Yud* and the *Nun*, is that the *Yud* elevates everything in this month. It elevates all the *Nuns*. All areas of our lives have the power to be elevated this month though the combination of the *Yud* and the *Nun*. This is the key for gaining the true freedom that awaits us in the month of Shevat.

As long as we are not free, as long as we are enslaved to our ego, to our *Desire to Receive for the Self Alone*, everything will affect and hinder us. So we have two powerful tools in this month. One is meditation on the letter Tzadi. The second is the simple principle of not being reactive to the ego that hopes to enslave us. This needs to be done, not because we want to be "nice" towards other people but because we want to escape bondage in all areas of our lives.

By using these tools we give ourselves the opportunity for true freedom. But if we focus our consciousness and desire for freedom on only one specific area, this opens us up to chaos in other areas of our lives. We need to say, "Yes, this is the area in which I need freedom today. But I also understand that my present need is only a manifestation of the chaos that has been present in my life and of the darkness that is in this world." Our consciousness must not be limited. We may need one aspect of freedom now, but our needs are sure to change as our spiritual work continues. Since our needs will change, it is change itself—or transformation—that is what we really require for ourselves. Transformation is what we should ask for, and transformation is what we should meditate upon.

This is a very important lesson for our spiritual work in this month. We may share, we may meditate, we may engage in many spiritual actions that have the ability to draw and reveal Light. But in addition to all the connections we make, we must break free from who we once were, and become who we are intended to be. If we do not do so, then the Light that is waiting to come down into our lives cannot manifest.

Often, we do things that have the power to bring abundance and peace into our lives, but we find, even after performing those actions, that we still have not seen any manifestation of the Light. In order for that manifestation to occur, real transformation has to happen within us. We can compare this to a person who makes a lot of money and puts it in his bank account. If he wants to buy a car, he has to take that money out of the bank and make the purchase. If he creates a tremendous bank account but never actually uses it, of course he'll still be lacking. He might even be starving!

The connection that comes to us this month provides us with an extra boost of energy that can eliminate many of our negative traits. Furthermore, we can tap into an awesome power that is unique to Shevat—the gift of freedom. But in order to truly understand what this gift is, we have to understand what freedom means. For some, it's political freedom. For others, it's more personal. Rav Ashlag, in his *Gift of the Bible*, goes into a complex explanation of freedom, or *herut* as *The Zohar* calls it. But no matter how we define freedom, one thing is certain: True freedom must involve complete and lasting freedom from chaos. Spiritual work is the first part of the process. It puts Light in our spiritual bank accounts, but that in itself is not enough to bring Light into our lives because all we have done is create a reservoir. We have to take the Light from those "bank accounts" and bring it into our lives, and the only way we can do that is through real transformation.

There's a story about a man who was in need of a loan. He went to a friend who was very wealthy and said, "I need this amount of money right now. I've come into hard times." The wealthy man said, "Certainly. Come to the bank tomorrow morning. I'll meet you at the front door." The next day the wealthy man was waiting at the bank, but when the borrower didn't appear, he waited an hour and then left.

That night, there was a knock on the wealthy man's door. It was his friend again, who said, "You know, I've come into hard times. Can you please lend me some money?" The wealthy man said in disbelief, "I told you yesterday I'm happy to lend you this money, and I waited for you at the bank." And the borrower replied, "Oh, you're right! I'm sorry! I forgot!"

So the next morning, the wealthy man was waiting at the bank, and again, his friend failed to show up. And the story keeps repeating itself.

The kabbalists explain that this is a very silly story, but it's no sillier than the way many of us live our lives. We perform those actions that have the potential to reveal a tremendous amount of Light. But if we don't transform ourselves, the Light cannot become manifest in our lives. So it's crucial that as we continue in our spiritual work, not just to focus on actions but also on true change within. This inner change is something that only we can know about ourselves. Only we can know that we didn't react when somebody cut us off on the highway. Only we can know that today when the boss said something unkind, it didn't even bother us. This is true change, and it's probably the most difficult thing for us to achieve. And that's one of the gifts of Shevat—that we can now understand that the true manifestation of blessings in our lives can occur only when we transform our nature.

CHAPTER 20

Rosh Chodesh Adar

The kabbalists teach that when the month of Adar (Pisces) begins, joy also begins. At its root, both the joy and the gift of Adar is our ability in this month to face our darkness and to dispel it. From this comes our ability to connect to the Light of the Creator and real joy.

Abraham the Patriarch, in his *Sefer Yetzirah*, *The Book of Formation*, teaches us that the letter *Kuf* created the month of Adar, so by understanding the essence of the letter *Kuf*, we can understand the gift of the month of Adar. *Kuf* is the only letter of the Hebrew alphabet that goes below the baseline of all the other letters. It takes us below the surface. It allows us to penetrate to the root of chaos, to the origin of the negativity that's all around us. *Kuf* is the only letter that provides us with an opportunity to invade the home territory of Satan.

The Tetragrammaton combination that is the channel for the Light of this month is *Hei, Hei, Yud,* and *Vav.* One reason this month's Tetragrammaton combination begins with a letter *Hei* followed by another letter *Hei* is to signify the cutting away of the *Kuf.* If we take the letter *Kuf* and remove the bottom half, that is, the part of the letter that goes below the line, we're left with the letter *Hei.* Because it contains both the energy of *Binah* and *Malchut, Hei* is a letter that is a complete channel for the Light of the Creator. So the process of the month of Adar is to take the letter *Kuf*—the darkness that is in every single one of us, the aspect of us that goes "below the line"—and cut it off at the level of *Malchut,* and then we will be able to connect to the Upper World of Binah.

One of the great gifts of Adar is the chance to develop the Light within ourselves, not by ignoring our darkness or trying to forget about it, but by really transforming it into Light. No matter how long we've been connected to negativity, no matter how many negative actions we've taken, every single one of us has Light behind the veil of darkness, and during Adar, we can change the darkness into Light just as we can change the *Kuf* into the *Hei.* Whether it is jealousy, anger, selfishness, or anything else that diminishes the Light and blessings we can draw into our lives, this month gives us the gift to remove those barriers.

Every other month of the year provides us with energy to create a security shield so that chaos cannot penetrate our environment. But the month of Adar allows us to actually invade the enemy's own territory. We actually attack what the Rav calls the "playing field of Satan."

When we move into the area where chaos originates, we understand that pain and suffering does not begin on the physical level. If someone offends us or causes us pain and we blame that person, we are not looking deep enough. We are simply staying within the confines of chaos, within the confines of negativity. We have to understand that we are the reason, we are the cause. As long as we continue to blame others for our problems, we are still stuck in chaos.

So the first tool we can use to extricate ourselves from chaos is an understanding that the reason for our pain will never be something external to us. If there is negativity in our life, it is because we personally have done something of a negative nature, and through that negative action, we have given energy to chaos. Then that negative energy rebounds on us via another person or situation.

According to the Rav, in order to remove energy from the root of chaos, we have to go beyond blame. This is the first step, the first level of consciousness: not only going into the playing field of Satan, but also beginning to eliminate the energy that we have given to chaos.

The second level of consciousness is that whenever a difficulty comes into our lives, we have to see it not as a problem, but as a stepping stone as well as a stronger connection to more Light. The Rav says that the consciousness of transforming darkness into Light at the root or seed level is not only important for ourselves as individuals, but is also important for the whole world. As this consciousness spreads throughout humankind, we can bring about the true, ultimate transformation that we all hope for.

Unfortunately, we too often underestimate the true power of our own souls and the Light that is within our souls. It's important that we understand the tremendous Light and the great power that lies in our souls. At the same time, it's also important to be aware that there is a darkness. There is a lack. There is the part of us that the kabbalists call the *Desire to Receive for the Self Alone*, which can take many forms and includes all our negative traits. Our inclination to speak badly of other people, our desire to inflict pain or sadness on other people—all of that negativity comes from a darkness that every single one of us has within ourselves. So we need to recognize both of these elements, the darkness *and* the tremendous Light, residing within our souls. Both of these aspects are very powerful. The sad reality is that we are often only dimly aware of the Light that we have within us, while at the same time we are often completely blind to the darkness that is also within us.

Even when we become involved in spiritual work and begin to make a connection with the Light, we may think that just by bringing more and more Light into ourselves, we can diminish the darkness. But that is not the case. Light and darkness, positive energy and negative energy can and do live at the same time within all of us.

Once we understand that Light and darkness can coexist within the same person, we're no longer shocked by people's negative actions—not even the negative actions of those who are studying Kabbalah and trying to connect with the Light. Still, we often try to ignore the negativity, both in others and especially in ourselves, because we're afraid. We believe that even acknowledging that we have negative thoughts or perform negative actions will make us "bad people," and therefore, whether subconsciously or consciously, we avoid delving into that darkness.

One of the ideas that this month teaches us is not to become discouraged by our own darkness. We are not "good" or "bad" people. We are not either Light or darkness. Every single one of us always has both aspects. We can act in the most negative of ways on any one day, but that does not mean that we're totally negative. The Light is still there. By the same token, there can be days when we perform genuinely sharing actions, but that doesn't mean that the darkness is no longer there.

The fact that we have tremendous Light at the same time that we have darkness means that we should not be frightened to look within ourselves. Only by truly recognizing those aspects of our lives—the actions, thoughts, and words that are of the darkness—only by delving into them, thinking about them, and consistently acknowledging them, can we truly remove them.

This is a very inspiring idea, and it calls to mind the story of Rav Chaim Vital and his teacher, Rav Isaac Luria (the Ari). During the years they spent together, Rav Chaim Vital, who was one of the greatest souls to ever come down to this world, had a tremendous problem controlling his anger. Regarding this, the Ari told Rav Vital, "The more you grow and the more connected you become to the Light of the Creator, the more difficult the darkness will become, and the more strongly you will have to fight your anger."

Every single one of us is in a similar position. This doesn't make us bad. It makes us human, and it gives us the ability to reveal even more Light in our lives.

In his book *Gift of the Bible*, the great kabbalists Rav Yehuda Ashlag explains that the only way we can erase our negative tendencies is to completely clarify them. He calls this the *koosh hakarat hara*, or our ability to look within ourselves and truly ascertain the aspects of our personality that are of darkness. Rav Ashlag makes the amazing point that our nature, our soul, our Light, is even greater than we can ever imagine. It has the ability to force the darkness out. But before that darkness and that negativity can be forced out, we have to bring it to the surface. We bring it to the surface by facing it, by thinking about it, and by truly owning the darkness in ourselves.

There is no greater spiritual tool to cleanse darkness and negativity than *The Zohar*. As Rav Chaim Vital writes, whenever anyone came to the Ari with a problem, whether it was jealousy, selfishness, anger, or anything else, the Ari would always say, "Read a certain number of pages in *The Zohar* every day. If you do that continuously and diligently, that darkness will vanish."

With this in mind, each of us during this month needs to do at least two things. First, we need to really look within ourselves and find those areas that are still in darkness. And let's not fool ourselves: We all have those areas. The greater the Light, the greater the darkness will often be. Then as we find those areas of darkness and focus on them, we must use *The Zohar* to cleanse them and take them away.

Often in life we have troubles. We have things that we worry about and that make us sad. But there's a great quote from one of the kabbalists: "You think that you have problems and therefore you're sad. But really, you're sad and therefore you have problems."

The Negative Side wants us to look at problems and become sad from them. By becoming sad, we restrict the amount of Light that can come into our lives. If we weren't restricting that Light, if we'd make the decision to be happy, many of those problems and worries would disappear.

One of the great gifts of Adar is that it is easier to be happy during this month if only we make that choice. In this month we can't hold onto our chaos. We cannot hold onto our sadness and our worries. There's a tremendous gift of joy in Adar and it's important that we connect to it. After all, who doesn't want to be happy?

This doesn't mean that we should ignore a problem if we have one. We should take care of it. But we should let go of the worry beforehand and the residue afterward because continually fixating on the problem simply mires us in a circle of darkness and sadness. In this month we have to make a decision that we are not going to allow anything to prevent our happiness, because Adar is a time of joy. To the degree that we awaken this joy, the more Light we will have, not only during Adar but in the whole year to come. The Light of the Creator, the tremendous blessings and abundance that we all want, can only come when we have a Vessel of happiness.

So it's not only that we don't want to be sad, it's that we *can't afford* to be sad. Sadness will diminish the blessings of this month as well as the blessings in our life overall. It's a simple decision we need to make: "I am not going to worry about or be afraid of those things. Never forget that darkness does not diminish by itself. We have to find the darkness and we have to deal with it. Through the power of this month, we can push darkness away. That is one gift of Adar.

The second gift of Adar is happiness itself. When the month of Adar, which is also the month of Pisces, begins, the gates of happiness open. We need to take advantage of this, not only because we want to be happy but because we want more Light. We want more abundance. So at the beginning of Adar we need to say, "This is the month that I'm going to dedicate to simple happiness." And as we create a Vessel of happiness, all the other blessings and all the other abundance will come. But it can happen only after we create the Vessel. All of us want to have joyful lives, but to be joyful is a choice we must make, a switch we must activate in our minds. There are many practical steps we can take to hit this switch, and they all involve finding the excitement and the beauty in the permanent and lasting gifts of the Light.

This month, practice starting each day with gratitude. As you open your eyes in the morning, focus on one thing you are grateful for. Choose a permanent aspect of your life when you do this, not some fleeting bit of excitement from the material world. Allow yourself to sink into the positive feelings that come up. Most importantly, don't get out of bed until you find something to be grateful for. Then as you go through the day, think often of this gratitude, keeping in mind that a new awareness of joy will not happen by itself.

Of course, the negativity within us will do everything possible to keep us in a reactive state. So be tenacious this month about thinking thoughts of joy and happiness. The more you do this, the more blessings you will see manifesting in your life. And when you need extra support, meditate on the Tetragrammaton combination for the month and on the letter *Kuf.*

Once and for all, at its core and its foundation, Adar is a month of joy. Most importantly, as we discussed earlier, we have the ability in this month to face our darkness—to face whatever it is that makes us diminish the Light and blessings that come into our lives and remove those blockages immediately.

What does this really mean?

Basically, there are two types of happiness: short-term excitement and long-term fulfillment. As we become more involved and more advanced in our spiritual work, it's important to realize that this work is never about having "less fun." Certainly in this month, the power of our spiritual connection means that we can be more filled with joy, more filled with happiness, more filled with fulfillment. Furthermore, it's important for us to also remember that this joy isn't only something that we want. It's something that we need, and something that we deserve.

CHAPTER 21

Purim

It is very important to appreciate the type of Light that is available on Purim. This explanation is a little bit technical because the more clarity we have about the spiritual process that occurred and is occurring now, the more Light we will connect to on Purim.

In *Gates of Meditation*, Rav Isaac Luria (the Ari) explains that there are five groupings within the *Ten Sfirot*, the spheres of emanation of the Tree of Life. The three upper *Sfirot* are *Keter*, *Chochmah* (our Supernal Father), and *Binah* (our Supernal Mother). Then, the next six *Sfirot* of *Chesed*, *Gvurah*, *Tiferet*, *Netzach*, *Hod*, and *Yesod*, combine together to form what the kabbalists call *Zeir Anpin*. Finally, we have the lowest *Sfirah* of *Malchut*, our physical world. We interact with the two lower levels: *Zeir Anpin* and *Malchut*, which have two basic positions: either face to face, the position that reveals the most Light; or back to back, where the least amount of Light is revealed. The Ari tells us that whenever people are forced into exile, *Zeir Anpin* and *Malchut* stand back to back.

The Ari teaches that the whole story of Purim—of Mordechai, Esther, King Achashverosh, and Haman—occurred toward the end of the seventy years of Israelite exile in Babylon. During this time of darkness, *Zeir Anpin* and *Malchut* stood back to back and thus separate from each other. In other words, there was a separation between the spiritual world (*Zeir Anpin*) and the physical world (*Malchut*). The kabbalistic teaching that *Zeir Anpin* was asleep is a metaphorical way of expressing this separation.

For *Zeir Anpin* and *Malchut* to turn face to face so that there could be a reconnection to the Light of the Creator, "surgery" was required to detach the one from the other. Before the surgery could take place, there had to be a process of sleeping, known by the kabbalists as *dormita*. While *Zeir Anpin* sleeps, meaning that the Light of *Zeir Anpin* is hidden from *Malchut*, the cutting away can occur. But there had to be this diminishment of Light in our world before the greater Light could be revealed. Indeed, the more darkness we experience, the greater the indication that we are getting closer to a great revelation of Light, which in this case was the end of the Babylonian exile. It's very important to understand, however, that this period of diminished Light in the world was a highly dangerous time.

In the Purim story, Haman intended to take advantage of this situation. Haman was not only an evil person but also a very wise one. His soul and the souls of his children literally came from the darkest part of the *klippot* (shells that capture and surround our Light). Through his knowledge of astrology, he understood what was taking place in the Upper Worlds. Haman saw that this was an opportune time to inflict damage and darkness upon the Israelites, who were unprotected because of the separation of *Zeir Anpin* and *Malchut*. To ensure the annihilation of the Israelites, Haman convinced King Achashverosh that they were a nation whose God was asleep. Haman explained to Achashverosh that if they ever wanted to succeed in creating and sustaining great darkness, now was the time.

But as the Ari explains, even while *Zeir Anpin* is asleep, *Malchut*, the female aspect, is not. What happens during the time of *dormita*, while *Zeir Anpin* is asleep, is that the Light leaves *Zeir Anpin* and enters *Malchut*. This occurs to prepare and help expand *Malchut* to receive the great amount of Light through the coming unification with *Zeir Anpin*.

Although the source of Light in the Upper Worlds (*Zeir Anpin*) was dormant, Mordechai represented the aspect of the physical world (*Malchut*) in which Light continued to manifest. Haman understood this, and his hatred of Mordechai was not simply the hatred of one person for another. Haman knew that Mordechai was the physical manifestation of great Light and could reconnect *Malchut* with *Zeir Anpin* even during the period while *Zeir Anpin* slept.

Haman's wife was also a great sorceress, and together they plotted to kill Mordechai in order to end his connection with the Light. If this plan had succeeded, it would have triggered disaster. The *only* connection in the world to the Light at this time was Mordechai. If Haman had been able to kill

Mordechai, all connection with the Light would have been lost, and Haman could have brought total chaos upon the world. To prevent this from happening, the Creator infused more Light into Mordechai and Esther so that the plan of Haman and Achashverosh did not succeed.

In kabbalistic terms, Mordechai was the Vessel into which Light from the Upper Worlds could flow. He was a Vessel built of our desire and our certainty that we can in fact draw the Light.

Knowledge of the Purim story is very important, as is the observance of the holiday itself. It is said that during the celebration of Purim, a person needs to get so drunk that he doesn't know the difference between Mordechai and Haman. This sounds like a joke, but it's actually a very wise teaching. The point is to elevate the Negative Side, to make it equal to and indistinguishable from the Light of the Creator.

This is a beautiful concept. As the Ari and Rav Ashlag explain in *Ten Luminous Emanations*, there is a level of being called *yuli* in Hebrew in which things exist before they become manifest. The only way to really change things is to take them back to this primal state, that is, before their defining characteristics appeared. This is what Esther did by inviting Haman to her dinner. Esther took the negativity embodied in Haman back to its unmanifested state. It is as if gold or silver coins were melted down so they could be re-formed in an entirely different configuration like a plate or piece of jewelry.

This is what we can accomplish at Purim: We can take all our negativity back to its unmanifested condition and reconstitute it. By taking that same energy back to the level of *yuli*, even a deeply negative action can become positive. It can be fundamentally changed. We can completely eradicate any negativity within us.

By studying the Purim story and by observing the ceremonies of the holiday, we can strengthen the Light that we can receive at this time. As part of our understanding of Purim, we need to realize that the Light revealed by Mordechai and Esther is sustained literally forever. To be able to sustain such a great revelation is something that does not occur any other time. Connection to the Light of Purim actually takes us to the time *after* the Final Redemption (*Gamar Hatikkun*). Even the greatest days of the year, such as Chanukah or Yom Kippur, connect us to only the moment of Redemption itself. Purim takes us even further, to a "time beyond time" when all other holidays will end. For this reason, the great kabbalist known as the Afta Rebbe taught that the energy of Purim is even stronger than that of Yom Kippur; in Hebrew, Yom Kippur is *Ki-Purim*, meaning "like Purim" or "almost as powerful as Purim."

To the degree that we understand the meaning of Purim, we will receive the timeless Light of Purim.

More from best-selling author Michael Berg

The Secret: Unlocking the Source of Joy & Fulfillment

The Secret reveals the essence of life in its most concise and powerful form. Several years before the latest "Secret" phenomenon, Michael Berg shared the amazing truths of the world's oldest spiritual wisdom in this book. In it, he has pieced together an ancient puzzle to show that our common understanding of life's purpose is actually backwards, and that anything less than complete joy and fulfillment can be changed by correcting this misperception.

Secrets of the Zohar: Stories and Meditations to Awaken the Heart

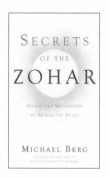

The Zohar's secrets are the secrets of the Bible, passed on as oral tradition and then recorded as a sacred text that remained hidden for thousands of years. They have never been revealed quite as they are here in these pages, which decipher the codes behind the best stories of the ancient sages and offer a special meditation for each one. Entire portions of the Zohar are presented, with the Aramaic and its English translation in side-by-side columns. This allows you to scan and to read aloud so that you can draw on the Zohar's full energy and achieve spiritual transformation. Open this book and open your heart to the Light of the Zohar!

Well of Life: Kabbalistic Wisdom from a Depth of Knowledge

Kabbalah teaches that portions of the Bible connect to distinct weekly energies, and tapping into those energies helps to connect us with the Light. Here, in 52 short chapters, corresponding to each week of the lunar year, Michael Berg decodes key stories from the Bible, revealing the lessons to be learned from them, and shows you how you can maximize each week's energy to create a more meaningful life.

Becoming Like God: Kabbalah and Our Ultimate Destiny

During the ten years that he worked on translating the 23 volumes of *The Zohar*, Michael Berg discovered the long-lost secret for which humanity has searched for more than 5,000 years: how to achieve our ultimate destiny. *Becoming Like God* reveals the transformative method by which people can actually break free of what is called "ego nature" to achieve total joy and lasting life.

Berg puts forth the revolutionary idea that we are ready for the next and final phase in human evolution: becoming like God.

More books that can help you bring the wisdom of Kabbalah into your life

Living Kabbalah: A Practical System for Making the Power Work for You
By Yehuda Berg

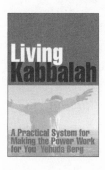

Living Kabbalah is a unique system of technology meant for you to use to transform your life and achieve true and lasting fulfillment. In these pages, you will find practical tools and exercises to help you break negative patterns, overcome challenges, and incorporate the time-tested wisdom of Kabbalah into your daily life. Noted author and teacher Yehuda Berg provides a clear blueprint that guides you step-by-step along the path toward the ultimate attainment of all that you need and desire.

Tap into a greater power—the power of Kabbalah—and learn to live more fully, richly, and joyfully every day, starting today!

The Prayer of the Kabbalist: The 42 - Letter Name of God
By Yehuda Berg

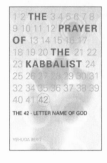

According to the ancient wisdom of Kabbalah, the powerful prayer known as *Ana Bekho'ah* invokes The 42-Letter Name of God, which connects to no less than the undiluted force of creation. By tapping into this connection through the Prayer, you can leave the past behind and make a fresh start. If you recite the Prayer on a regular basis, you are able to use the force of creation to create miracles, both in your everyday life and in the world at large. This book explains the meaning behind the 42 letters and gives you practical steps for how best to connect to their power.

Immortality: The Inevitability of Eternal Life
By Rav Berg

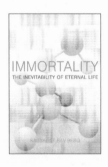

This book will totally change the way in which you perceive the world, if you simply approach its contents with an open mind and an open heart.

Most people have it backwards, dreading and battling what they see as the inevitability of aging and death. But, according to the great Kabbalist Rav Berg and the ancient wisdom of Kabbalah, it is eternal life that is inevitable.

With a radical shift in our cosmic awareness and the transformation of the collective consciousness that will follow, we can bring about the demise of the death force once and for all— in this "lifetime."

God Wears Lipstick: Kabbalah for Women
By Karen Berg

For thousands of years, women were banned from studying Kabbalah, the ancient source of wisdom that explains who we are and what our purpose is in this universe. Karen Berg changed that. She opened the doors of The Kabbalah Centre to all who would seek to learn.

In God Wears Lipstick, Karen Berg shares the wisdom of Kabbalah, especially as it affects you and your relationships. She reveals a woman's special place in the universe and why women have a spiritual advantage over men. She explains how to find your soulmate and your purpose in life, and empowers you to become a better human being.

The Power of Kabbalah

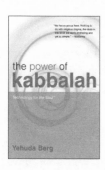

Imagine your life filled with unending joy, purpose, and contentment. Imagine your days infused with pure insight and energy. This is *The Power of Kabbalah*. It is the path from the momentary pleasure that most of us settle for, to the lasting fulfillment that is yours to claim. Your deepest desires are waiting to be realized. Find out how, in this basic introduction to the ancient wisdom of Kabbalah.

The Zohar

Composed more than 2,000 years ago, the *Zohar* is a set of 23 books, a commentary on biblical and spiritual matters in the form of conversations among spiritual masters. But to describe the *Zohar* only in physical terms is greatly misleading. In truth, the *Zohar* is nothing less than a powerful tool for achieving the most important purposes of our lives. It was given to all humankind by the Creator to bring us protection, to connect us with the Creator's Light, and ultimately to fulfill our birthright of true spiritual transformation.

More than eighty years ago, when The Kabbalah Centre was founded, the *Zohar* had virtually disappeared from the world. Few people in the general population had ever heard of it. Whoever sought to read it—in any country, in any language, at any price—faced a long and futile search.

Today all this has changed. Through the work of The Kabbalah Centre and the editorial efforts of Michael Berg, the *Zohar* is now being brought to the world, not only in the original Aramaic language but also in English. The new English *Zohar* provides everything for connecting to this sacred text on all levels: the original Aramaic text for scanning; an English translation; and clear, concise commentary for study and learning.

The Kabbalah Centre

The International Leader in the Education of Kabbalah

Since its founding, The Kabbalah Centre has had a single mission: to improve and transform people's lives by bringing the power and wisdom of Kabbalah to all who wish to partake of it.

Through the lifelong efforts of Kabbalists Rav and Karen Berg, and the great spiritual lineage of which they are a part, an astonishing 3.5 million people around the world have already been touched by the powerful teachings of Kabbalah. And each year, the numbers are growing!

. . . .

If you were inspired by this book in any way and would like to know how you can continue to enrich your life through the wisdom of Kabbalah, here is what you can do next:

Call 1-800-KABBALAH where trained instructors are available 18 hours a day. These dedicated people are willing to answer any and all questions about Kabbalah and help guide you along in your effort to learn more.

The Kabbalah Action Group would like to dedicate this book to all its members and to those whose lives have been touched by the wisdom passed down by the Kabbalists. We are grateful for the opportunity to share with the world the life-changing wisdom of Kabbalah taught by the Rav and Karen, Michael and Yehuda Berg, and all the teachers of The Kabbalah Centre.

Enjoy this book, and if its words, indeed, touch your heart, please share it with your friends, family, and community.